CONTRACT L.
Q&A

Private Law Tutor Publishing
Foreword

Thank you for buying this book. The problem that I encountered when studying law is: knowing everything. There is so much to read and so little time to do it. If you skip some material, or a case you are none the wiser. So throughout my years teaching law I have devised a system and I am going to share this with you.

You may have encountered different methods or formulas to help when advising a client in a mock scenario. One of example is the *IRAC* method or another is *Celo*. These are well documented and you can read about these. I never used them, because I had a method in my head that worked. It was not until I started teaching that I spoke about it. I call my method the "Fact Law Sandwich". Let me explain. If you are asked to advise a party as to their legal rights this is how you present it:

FACTS
GENERAL PRINCIPLE
LAW
APPLY TO FACTS

In **Fact:** simply state what you have been told, this why you can never be accused of not considering the facts. In **General principle:** you simply state what the general rule of the relevant issue is. You express it as if you are speaking to a child who has no knowledge of law. In **Law**: you state "using the authority of.....and you go on to state which statute or case helps prove your point. Lastly in **Apply to Facts**: you apply the reasoning of the case to your factual scenario. Your advice will sound and look structured and professional. The reason it is called the "Fact Law Sandwich", is because the advice contains two outer layers of facts that sandwich the principle and law in the middle.

This book is written to provide the student with a good knowledge of the most important cases on their study. It is written in a way to facilitate the Fact Law Sandwich method. I provide the general principle, the name of the case with full citation, the facts, the Ratio (the thing the lecturers say you always need to use), and application i.e. how the case should be applied. No other book provides this information at your fingertips. I hope you enjoy using it.

CONTRACT LAW Q&As

Private Law Tutor Publishing

Chapter 1 - Introduction/Overview

Chapter 2 and 3 – offer/Acceptance/Revocation
Question and Answers
- Offer and Acceptance problem 1
- Offer and Acceptance Problem 2
- Battle of the Forms Essay
- Postal Rule and Instantaneous Communication Essay

Chapter 4 - Consideration
Question and Answers
- Consideration Essay Question
- Consideration Problem Question

Chapter 5 – Duress
Question and Answer
- Duress Essay Question

Chapter 6 – Promissory Estoppel
Question and Answer
- Promissory Estoppel Essay

Chapter 7 - Intention to Create Legal Relations
Question and Answer
- Problem Question Intention to Create Legal Relations

Chapter 8- Privity of Contract
Question and Answer
- Privity of Contract Problem Question

Chapter 9 - Terms of the Contract
Question and Answers
- Problem question on Implied Terms
- Terms of Contract Essay Question

- Terms of Contract Problem Question

Chapter 10 - Exemption Clauses
Question and Answers
- Unfair Contract Terms Act 1979 Essay
- Exclusion clause Problem Question

Chapter 11 – Misrepresentation
Question and Answer
- Misrepresentation Problem Question

Chapter 12 - Mistake
Question and Answer
- Mistake Problem Question

Chapter 13 - Remedies
Question and Answers
- Remedies Problem Question

Chapter 1 - Welcome/Introduction/Overview

This book provides you with basic information as a basis for you to form your own critical opinions on this area of law. Once you have mastered the basics, you will be inspired to question contract principles in your essays and apply them in mock client advisory scenarios. Again, for your convenience, we have provided you with examples of how to answer such questions and how to apply your knowledge as effectively as possible to help you get the best possible marks.

This aid is a fully-fledged source of basic information, which tries to give the student comprehensive understanding for this module. However, it is recommended that you compliment it with the further reading suggestions provided at the end of each topic, as well as read the cases themselves for more in-depth information. This book provides an analysis of the basic principles of modern Contract Law. The following is a summary of the Book content:

- An introduction to the Law of Contract;
- How contracts are formed;
- What goes into a contract: Its content;
- The means of obtaining remedies when there is a breach of contract;

The aim of this Book is to:

- Provide an introduction to anyone studying or interested in studying Law to the key principles and concepts that exist in the Law of Contract.
- To provide a framework to consider Contract Law within the context of examinations.
- Provide a detailed learning resource in order for legal written examination skills to be developed.
- Facilitate the development of written and critical thinking skills.
- Promote the practice of problem solving skills.
- To establish a platform for students to gain a solid

understanding of the basic principles and concepts of Contract Law, this can then be expanded upon through confident independent learning.

Through this Book, students will be able to demonstrate the ability to:

- Demonstrate an awareness of the core principles of Contract Law.
- Critically assess challenging mock factual scenarios and be able to pick out legal issues in the various areas of Contract Law.
- Apply their knowledge when writing a formal assessment.
- Present a reasoned argument and make a judgment on competing viewpoints.
- Make use of technical legalistic vocabulary in the appropriate manner.
- Be responsible for their learning process and work in an adaptable and flexible way.

Studying Contract Law

Contract is one of the seven core subjects that the Law Society and the Bar Council deem essential in a qualifying law degree. Therefore, it is vital that a student successfully pass this subject to become a lawyer. Additionally, a knowledge and understanding of contractual principles is needed in order to study other law subjects such as company, employment, international trade, commercial, or even family law. The primary method by which your understanding of the law of contract will develop is by understanding how to solve problem questions. You will also be given essay questions in your examinations. The methods by which these types of question should be approached are somewhat different.

Tackling Problems and Essay Questions

There are various ways of approaching problem questions and essay questions. We have provided students with an in-depth analysis with suggested questions and answers at the end of each chapter.

Chapter 2 and 3 - Offer and Acceptance and Revocation

Questions and Answers

- Offer and Acceptance problem 1
- Offer and Acceptance Problem 2
- Battle of the forms essay
- Postal rule and instantaneous communication essay

Offer and Acceptance Problem Question One

On 9th December 2009, Abdul placed a notice on the University noticeboard as follows:

"Second-hand computer. Good condition. Worth £1,000. Selling for £175. Will sell to the first person to notify me by 13th January 2010. Telephone: 020 7320 9876. Email abdul0231@xyz.com Address: 1A, High Street, New Town, London E1."

Samson posted a letter on 8th January 2010, by first class recorded delivery post, agreeing to buy the computer for £175. Owing to the negligence of the Post Office, the letter was delivered to Abdul only on 14th January 2010.

Diana read the notice, telephoned Abdul on 12th January and left a message on his answer-phone, agreeing to buy the computer for £175. She also asked whether she could pay for the computer when she received her student loan money. Abdul listened to this message only on 14th January.

Maggie sent an email on 10th January, agreeing to buy the computer for £175. Abdul read the email on the 12th and sent a reply to Maggie, giving her an appointment to collect the computer on 16th January at 8 pm. Maggie responded by email, saying that she would pay the money when she collects the computer.

On 16th January, a leading computer shop in London decides to do a clearance sale and is selling good, brand new computers at £150 each.

Samson, Diana, and Maggie no longer wish to buy Abdul's computer.

Advise Abdul whether Samson, Diana and Maggie are under a contractual obligation to buy his computer.

Offer and Acceptance Problem Question One: Answer

Introduction

This paper is an advice for Abdul, Samson, Diana and Maggie in relation to the recent negotiation in relation to the sale of the computer. First, this paper will advise the parties as to whether a legally enforceable contact has been formed. The paper will do this by advising on the issue of the advertisement, and whether this will be viewed by the courts as a unilateral offer or an invitation to treat. Second, this paper will discuss the issue of Samson's acceptance by post, using the relevant case law. Third, this paper will discuss the issue of whether Diana's message was capable of acceptance. Fourth, this paper will critically discuss whether Maggie's acceptance through email was valid. Lastly, this paper will conclude its findings.

Unilateral offer or invitation to treat

For a contract to exist one party ("the offeror") needs to make a clear and certain offer and the other party (the offeree) needs to communicate their equally clear and unequivocal acceptance. It is important to establish whether the advertisement placed on the notice board is an invitation to treat or an offer. If it is an offer, it will be capable of being accepted by the parties. However, if it is an invitation to treat, the parties must make the offer to Abdul, who may then choose to accept or reject it.

On 9th December 2009, Abdul, placed a notice on the University notice board as follows: *"Second-hand computer. Good condition. Worth £1,000. Selling for £175. Will sell to the first person to notify me by 13th January 2010. Telephone: 020 7320 9876. Email abdul0231@xyz.com Address: 1A, High Street, New Town, London E1."*

Generally, advertisements are regarded by the courts as statements inviting further negotiations or invitations to treat. An example of this was seen in **Partridge v Crittenden**[1] where a notice reading *'Bramblefinch cocks and hens, 25s each'* was placed in the classified advertisement page of a periodical. The Court of Appeal held that newspaper advertisements are ordinarily to be treated as invitations to treat and not offers. The logic of this decision was set out by Lord Parker CJ, who noted the *"business sense in* [advertisements] *being construed as invitations to treat and not as offers"*[2]. Moreover, Lord Parker CJ in agreement cited Lord Herschell in ***Grainger & Son v Gough***[3], where he made the point that it would be wrong to regard these types of advertisements as offers because *"the merchant might find himself involved in any number of contractual obligations to supply wine of a particular description which he would be quite unable to carry out,"* because the merchant would have a limited supply.

A possible line of argument that might be raised by the parties is that this advertisement constitutes a unilateral contract. A unilateral offer is where one party makes an offer or proposal, which is open to the world and is capable of acceptance by anyone. The other party 'accepts' the offer by performing the act in accordance with the requirements of the offer. Using **Carlill v Carbolic Smoke Ball Co.**[4], which is the authority on unilateral contracts, it can be argued the advertisement is in very firm terms and because the price and description of the computer are stated, it requires no further negation and is capable of being accepted by performance of payment. The advertisement states Abdul "[w]*ill sell to the first person to notify* [him] *by 13th January 2010"*. This may be interpreted by the court to be a unilateral offer.

However, the opposing argument to this can be drawn from what was argued by Finlay, Q.C., and T. Terrell for the defendant Smoke ball company in **Carlill** that *"the offer, the terms of which are too vague to be treated as a definite offer"*[5]. This argument is on a balance of probabilities likely to prevail because the

---

[1] [1968] 1 WLR 1204
[2] Partridge v Critenden [1986] 1 WLR 1204 per Lord Parker para 1209
[3] [1896] AC 325
[4] (1893) 1 QB 256
[5] (1893) 1 QB 256 at p 257

10

advertisement is not clear, precise and unequivocal. For example, although the advertisement has a good description of the computer, it lacks information about the way in which acceptance should take place through performance or the way in which payment should be made, i.e. how is Abdul to be contracted. It is, therefore, merely an invitation to treat and not an offer. This means that the parties must make the offer to Abdul, who can choose to accept or reject it.

Furthermore, Abdul is stipulating when acceptance must take place. This would suggest the offer is only open until *13th January 2010* and will lapse after this time. The leading case on this point is **Ramsgate Victoria Hotel Co. v Montefiore,** in which the courts stated, even an offer that has not been formally withdrawn would expire after "a reasonable time". In this case, the offer was for the sale of shares and the court felt six months was beyond what was reasonable.

Samson

Samson has posted a letter on 8th January 2010 by first class recorded delivery post, agreeing to buy the computer for £175. Owing to the negligence of the Post Office, the letter was delivered to Abdul only on 14th January 2010. If the advert is deemed a unilateral offer, then acceptance is normally effectual and the contract binding once acceptance is received by the offeror. However, the courts have introduced the postal rule to overcome the problem of the time a letter spends in the postal system. The problem with the postal system is that it creates a period of uncertainty for the parties, because the offeror is unaware if the offer has been accepted and the offeree is unaware whether the offer has been revoked. The postal rule was laid down in **Adams v Lindsell**. [6] Where post is deemed to be the proper means of communication, the acceptance takes effect from the moment the letter of acceptance is properly posted.

We are not told whether the post was Abdul's preferred method

---

[6] (1818) 1 B & Ald 681

of communication. It would appear the postal rule that applies Samson's acceptance is valid, even though it was only read by Abdul on 14th January 2010. An illustration of this was seen in **Henthorn v Fraser**.[7] Fraser offered, in writing, to sell certain houses to Henthorn, with the offer to remain open for 14 days. Henthorn received the offer in person. The next day, at midday, the society posted a letter to Henthorn revoking the offer. At 3:50pm, Henthorn posted a letter to the society accepting the offer. At 5:00pm, Henthorn received the society's revocation. The court in this case held a contract was made at 3:50pm when Henthorn posted his letter of acceptance.

Therefore, applying both cases above, it would appear Samson has benefited under the postal rule and accepted the offer and has a binding contract. However, the lawyers for Abdul may alternatively argue that Samson should not be allowed to benefit under the postal rule and there is no binding agreement, because the advert was at all times an invitation to treat; therefore, his letter will be construed as an offer. The authority for this proposition is **Thornton v Shoe Lane Parking Ltd**[8], which concerned the purchase of a ticket from the machine where he parked his car. In this case, Lord Denning went to great lengths to describe where an offer takes place and where an acceptance takes place.

Diana

Diana read the notice, telephoned Abdul on 12th January and left a message on his answer-phone, agreeing to buy the computer for £175, but asked whether she could pay for the computer when she received her student loan money. Abdul listened to this message only on 14th January. Again, if the advertisement is deemed invitation to treat using **Thornton v Shoe Lane Parking Ltd**, Diana's telephone call will be an offer, which Abdul can choose to accept or reject. If the court views this as a unilateral contract, then the offer of £175 could be a binding acceptance.

---

[7] [1892] 2 Ch 27
[8] [1971] 2 QB 163

However, a reason why there is no binding acceptance is because acceptance must communicated. Here, Abdul listened to this message only on 14th January once the offer had expired. The onus is on Diana to communicate acceptance. This principle is found in the case of **Entores v Miles Far East** [9] where Lord Denning said:

> *"Suppose, for instance, that I shout an offer to a man across a river or a courtyard but I do not hear his reply because it is drowned by an aircraft flying overhead. There is no contract at that moment. If he wishes to make a contract, he must wait till the aircraft is gone and then shout back his acceptance so that I can hear what he says. Not until I have his answer am I bound."* [10]

Another reason why the courts will not submit to the view that this is a unilateral offer and Diana's message is a valid acceptance is because Diana has varied the contract by asking for late payment. One of the general principles in contract law is that the acceptance must mirror the offer. The "mirror image rule" stipulates that, if Diana wants to accept the offer, she must accept an offer *exactly*, without any modifications; because Diana has changed the offer, this hypothetically becomes a counter-offer that kills the original offer, as seen in the case of **Hyde v. Wrench**.[11] Therefore, we are left in the same position that Diana's message is an offer that Abdul can either accept or reject. Diana may argue that this was only a request for further information as in **Stevenson v McLean**, in which the judge said there was no counter-offer, merely an enquiry that should have been answered. This line of argument is unlikely to succeed, however, because in **Stevenson v McLean**, a variation of delivery was sought. Here, there is late payment that is varying the contract.

Maggie

Maggie sent an email on 10th January agreeing to buy the

---

[9] [1955] 2 Q.B. 327
[10] [1955] 2 Q.B. 327 at 332
[11] (1840) 3 Beav 334

computer for £175. The advertisement is deemed a unilateral offer that will be binding. However, this is unlikely because it may have already have been sold. Thus, Maggie's email will be an offer. Abdul read the email on the 12th with the prescribed period of acceptance **Ramsgate Victoria Hotel Co. v Montefiore** and sent a reply to Maggie giving her an appointment to collect the computer on 16th January at 8 pm. This can be seen as the acceptance of the offer. **Thornton v Shoe Lane Parking Ltd.** Maggie responded by email, saying that she will pay the money when she collects the computer, which can be seen as an acknowledgement of the acceptance.

Conclusion

Abdul has no contract with Samson because he should not be allowed to benefit under the postal rule, and there is no binding agreement because the advert was at all times an invitation to treat. Abdul has no contract with Diana because acceptance must communicated by Diana. Here, Abdul listened to this message only on 14th January once the offer had expired. Also, Diana varied the offer and made a counter offer. Abdul has a binding contact with Maggie.

Offer and Acceptance Problem Question Two

On Monday, Golden Antiques places the following advertisement on their website: 'For sale, three Victorian style beds, gorgeous, £5000 each, cash, will brighten up any bed room!'

David, the manager of White Halls Ltd. Email Golden Antiques, immediately replies: 'White Halls Ltd. Will buy all three beds at £4500 each, please advise if credit facility is available'.

On Tuesday morning, Golden Antiques replies by email to say, 'We are not prepared to sell for less than £5000 each. Credit facility only available if your grantor is acceptable to us. Please confirm by close of business today if interested'.

On Tuesday afternoon, David faxes Golden Antiques to say he is willing to accept their original terms and will buy all three beds at £5000 each. He also faxes a letter he receives from Black Halls Ltd. (the guarantor) which states: 'It is our policy to ensure that our subsidiary, White Halls Ltd., remain solvent at all times". However, the fax was not properly transmitted, as indicated by the status report. David then posts a letter at 5pm accepting Golden Antiques' terms on Tuesday evening, although he knows there is a postal strike that day.

Roger, an accountant, telephones Golden Antiques on Wednesday morning stating that he wants to buy Victorian beds. He persuades the manager of Golden Antiques to sell the beds to him, on the basis that he had prepared the financial accounts for Golden Antiques the year before for half the fee he normally charges. Golden Antiques agrees to sell to Roger, so they send David a fax on Wednesday evening saying that the beds are no longer available for sale.

Golden Antiques receive David's letter at 3.45pm on Thursday. David does not read the fax from Golden Antiques until 4.00pm on Thursday.

Advise the parties as to their legal positions.

Offer and Acceptance Problem Question Two: Answer

Introduction

This paper is an advice for Golden Antiques, David, the manager of White Halls Ltd., and Roger, the accountant, ("the parties") in relation to the recent negotiation regarding the sale of three Victorian style beds. This paper will advise the parties as to whether a legally enforceable contact has been formed. The paper will do this by first, advising on the issue of the advertisement, and whether this will be viewed by the courts as a unilateral offer or an invitation to treat. Second, this paper will advise whether a valid offer has been made by Golden Antiques. Third, this paper will critically discuss whether David's acceptance through fax was valid. Fourth, this paper will critically discuss the issue of David's acceptance by post, using the relevant case law. Fifth, this paper will discuss the issue of the sale of the beds to Roger and whether this agreement provided the necessary consideration. Sixth, this paper will discuss whether Golden Antiques revocation took place before David's acceptance. Lastly, this paper will conclude its findings.

Unilateral offer or invitation to treat

For a contract to exist one party ("the offeror") needs to make a clear and certain offer and the other party (the offeree) needs to communicate their equally clear and unequivocal acceptance. It is important to establish whether the advertisement placed on their website is an invitation to treat or an offer. If it is an offer, it will be capable of being accepted by David. However, if it is an invitation to treat, David must make the offer to Golden Antiques who may then choose to accept or reject it. On Monday, Golden Antiques places the following advertisement on their website *'For sale, three Victorian style beds, gorgeous, £5000 each, cash, will brighten up any bed room!'*.

Generally advertisements are regarded by the courts as statements inviting further negotiations or invitations to treat. An example of this was seen in **Partridge v Crittenden**[12], where a notice reading 'Bramblefinch cocks and hens, 25s each' was placed in the classified advertisement page of a periodical. The Court of Appeal held that newspaper advertisements are ordinarily to be treated as invitations to treat and not offers. The logic of this decision was set out by Lord Parker CJ who noted the *"business sense in [advertisements] being construed as invitations to treat and not as offers"*[13]. Moreover, Lord Parker CJ in agreement cited Lord Herschell in ***Grainger & Son v Gough***[14], where he made the point that it would be wrong to regard these types of advertisements as offers because *"the merchant might find himself involved in any number of contractual obligations to supply wine of a particular description which he would be quite unable to carry out,"*, because the merchant would have a limited supply. Ewan Mckendrick points out *"this argument is not conclusive because it could be implied that the offer is only capable of acceptance while stocks last".*[15]

A possible line of argument that might be raised by Golden Antiques is that this advertisement constitutes a unilateral contract.[16] A unilateral offer is where one party makes an offer or proposal that is open to the world and capable of acceptance by anyone. The other party 'accepts' the offer by performing the act in accordance with the requirements of the offer. Using **Carlill v Carbolic Smoke Ball Co.,**[17] which is the authority on unilateral contracts, it can be argued the advertisement is in very firm terms, and because the price and description of the bed is stated, it requires no further negation and is capable of being accepted by performance of payment.[18]

However, the opposing argument to this can be drawn from what

---

[12] [1968] 1 WLR 1204
[13] Partridge v Critenden [1986] 1 WLR 1204 per Lord Parker para 1209
[14] [1896] AC 325
[15] Mckendrick E, Contract Law, Palgrove Macmillan Law Masters 7th Ed
[16] G.H. Treitel, The Law of Contract, 11th ed
[17] (1893) 1 QB 256
[18] G.H. Treitel, The Law of Contract, 11th ed

was argued by Finlay, Q.C., and T. Terrell for the defendant Smoke ball company in **Carlill** that *"the offer, the terms of which are too vague to be treated as a definite offer"*[19]. This argument is on a balance of probabilities likely to work because the advertisement is not clear, precise and unequivocal. For example, although the advertisement has a good description of the bed, it lacks information about the way in which acceptance should take place or the way in which payment should be made. It is, therefore, merely an invitation to treat and not an offer. This means that David must make the offer to Golden Antiques who can choose to accept or reject it.

A valid offer?

David is the manager of White Halls Ltd. and is acting in his capacity of agent for the White Halls Ltd. He has emailed Golden Antiques saying: *'White Halls Ltd. Will buy all three beds at £4500 each, please advise if credit facility is available'*. It is likely the advertisement is an invitation to treat; therefore, his email will be construed as an offer to Golden Antiques.

Another reason why the courts will not submit to the view that this is a unilateral offer and David's email is a valid acceptance is because David has varied the price of each bed to £4,500. One of the general principles in contract law is that the acceptance must mirror the offer. The "mirror image rule" stipulates that, if David wants to accept Golden Antiques offer, he must accept an offer *exactly*, without any modifications;[20] because David has changed the offer, this hypothetically becomes a counter-offer that kills the original offer, as seen in the case of **Hyde v. Wrench**.[21] Therefore, we are left in the same position that David's email is an offer that Golden Antiques can either accept or reject.

On Tuesday, Golden Antiques replies by email *'We are not prepared to sell for less than £5000 each.* This can be interpreted as a firm refusal by Golden Antiques of the offer presented by

---

[19] (1893) 1 QB 256 at p 257
[20] Mckendrick E, Contract Law, Palgrove Macmillan Law Masters 7th Ed
[21] (1840) 3 Beav 334

David. They have reaffirmed the price of the bed being £5,000. Using the authority of **Hyde v. Wrench** Golden Antiques have made a counter-offer which can now be accepted or rejected by David. Golden Antiques email further reads: *Credit facility only available if your grantor is acceptable to us.'* The statement about the credit facility is quite ambiguous because of the use of the phrase '*if your grantor is acceptable to us*'. Golden Antiques have not specified what the criteria are for the grantor to be acceptable. Lastly, the email reads: '*Please confirm by close of business today if interested'.* Golden Antiques are stipulating by when acceptance must take place. This would suggest the offer is only open for one day and will lapse at close of business. The leading case on this point is **Ramsgate Victoria Hotel Co. v Montefiore**[22], in which the courts said even if an offer has not been formally withdrawn, it would expire after "a reasonable time". In this case, the offer was for the sale of shares and the court felt six months was beyond what was reasonable.

The statement *'please advise if credit facility is available'* will be seen by the courts as a request for further information. Similarly in **Stevenson, Jacques & Co. v McLean**[23], when a customer asked for delivery over two months the courts held the plaintiff had not made a counter-offer but had made a mere enquiry which did not serve to reject the offer. A binding contract had been made when the plaintiffs sent the telegram accepting the offer.

David's acceptance through fax

On Tuesday afternoon, David faxes Golden Antiques to say he is willing to accept their original terms and will buy all three beds at £5000 each. David is accepting Golden Antiques offer, but the fax was not properly transmitted, as indicated by the status report. The general principle in contract law is that the acceptance must be communicated to the offeror. This principle is found in the case of **Entores v Miles Far East** [24], where Lord Denning said:

---

[22] (1866) LR 1 Ex 109
[23] (1880) 5 QBD 346
[24] [1955] 2 Q.B. 327

20

> *"Suppose, for instance, that I shout an offer to a man across a river or a courtyard but I do not hear his reply because it is drowned by an aircraft flying overhead. There is no contract at that moment. If he wishes to make a contract, he must wait till the aircraft is gone and then shout back his acceptance so that I can hear what he says. Not until I have his answer am I bound."*[25]

Furthermore, in **Brinkibon v Stahag Stahl**[26], Lord Wilberforce suggested there was no general rule that could cover all the possible situations in these types of cases. He added each case should be resolved with reference to the intention of the parties, to sound business practice, and, in some cases, to a judgment as to where the risks should lie. The case of Entores suggests that acceptance should take place only upon receipt of the fax. Therefore, the onus is on David to retransmit the fax until he is sure that Golden Antiques have received his acceptance. Failing this, there is no valid or enforceable contract between David and Golden Antiques.

David's acceptance by post

David then posts a letter at 5pm accepting Golden Antiques' terms on Tuesday evening; although he knows there is a postal strike that day. Acceptance is normally effectual and the contract binding once acceptance is received by the offeror. However, the courts have introduced the postal rule to overcome the problem of the time a letter spends in the postal system. The reason for this rule is to facilitate business and *"promote certainly within contractual formation at a time when the principle method of communication was slow"*.[27]

The postal rule was laid down in **Adams v Lindsell**.[28] Where post is deemed to be the proper means of communication, the

---

[25] [1955] 2 Q.B. 327 at 332
[26] [1982] 1 All ER 293
[27] Capps D, 'You've got Mail' 153 New Law Journal 906
[28] (1818) 1 B & Ald 681

acceptance takes effect from the moment the letter of acceptance is properly posted. We are not told whether the post was Golden Antiques preferred method of communication. But, because David has failed to successfully send the fax, he has opted for the post as a method of acceptance. An illustration of this was seen in **Henthorn v Fraser**.[29] The court, in this case, held a contract was made at 3:50pm when Henthorn posted his letter of acceptance.

Therefore, applying both cases above, it would appear David has benefited under the postal rule and accepted the offer and has a binding contract. However, the lawyers for Golden Antiques may alternatively argue that David should not be allowed to benefit under the postal rule and there is no binding agreement for two reasons:

First, the offer has lapsed under the **Ramsgate Victoria Hotel Co. v Montefiore**.[30] Golden Antiques stated in their email *'Please confirm by close of business today if interested'*. David had posted the letter at the close of business i.e. 5 o'clock. Thus the acceptance has come a moment too late. Another case which could be used in support of this argument (although this concerns telex and is not directly relevant) is **Tenax Steamship v The Brimnes (The Brimnes)** [31], where Cairns LJ felt that the sender should not rely on the recipients' reading every communication at once, and that, in some circumstances, a notice arriving late in the working day might quite legitimately not be "received" until the following morning.

Second, it could be argued that, because David knows there is a postal strike that day, it would be wrong to allow the postal rule to operate in this way. Lawton LJ in **Holwell Securities v Hughes** [32] seemed to support this proposition, when he said that the rule will not be applied where it would lead to: *'a manifest inconvenience and absurdity.'*[33] However, in the absence of

---

[29] [1892] 2 Ch 27
[30] (1866) LR 1 Ex 109
[31] [1974] 3 All ER 88
[32] [1974] 1 WLR 155
[33] [1974] 1 WLR 155 at 161

authority on this point, the courts may feel it right to allow the postal rule to apply.

Sale of the beds to Roger

Roger, an accountant, telephones Golden Antiques on Wednesday morning stating that he wants to buy Victorian beds. He persuades the manager of Golden Antiques to sell the beds to him, on the basis that he had prepared the financial accounts for Golden Antiques the year before for half the fee he normally charges. Golden Antiques agrees to sell to Roger. This is a breach of contract because the contract with David is binding if the postal rule applies.

If Golden Antiques want to change their mind and ultimately sell to David, they are able to do so, because the contract with Rodger may be unenforceable due to lack of consideration. The classic definition of consideration, found in the case of **Currie v Misa**,[34] is that consideration, *'may consist either in some right, interest, profit, or benefit accruing to the one party, or some forbearance, detriment, loss, or responsibility given, suffered, or undertaken by the other'*. This means Roger must provide something in return of the beds, i.e. money. We are told *'the manager of Golden Antiques to sell the beds to him'*. If Roger has paid money, this will be valid consideration.[35] If, however, Roger has not paid any money for the beds and he is relying on the fact he had prepared the financial accounts for Golden Antiques the year before for half the fee he normally charges, this will not be valid consideration for two reasons:

First, consideration must not be past. It is not possible to use consideration as some act that has taken place *prior* to the contract. Consideration must be given *in return* for the beds. This is a matter of fact and it is unlikely that the earlier work done at a discount by Roger will be valid consideration as payment for the beds. The discount was provided probably in order to secure the

---

[34] (1875) LR 10 Ex 153 per Lush J
[35] Chappell v Nestlé [1959] 2 All ER 701

work rather than as consideration for the future.

The general rule that consideration cannot be past was illustrated in **Eastwood v Kenyon**[36]. In this case, it was held a promise was insufficient where the consideration was wholly past. Moreover, in ***Roscorla v Thomas***[37], Roscorla bought Thomas' horse for £30. After the sale, Thomas promised Roscorla that the horse was sound and free from vice. The horse proved to be vicious. The court held there was no consideration to support Thomas' promise and he was not bound. The sale itself could not be valuable consideration, for it was completed prior to the promise being given.

However, in Roger's case, it can be argued that, because this is a transaction of a commercial nature, an implied promise to pay arises. This was acknowledged in the case of **Re Casey's Patents**[38], where the owners of patent rights promised their manager a share in those rights as consideration for his previous services for them. Bowen LJ said,

> *'The fact of a past service raises an implication that at the time it was rendered it was to be paid for, and, if it was a service which was to be paid for, when you get in a subsequent document a promise to pay, that promise may be treated as an admission which evidences or as a positive bargain which fixes the amount of that reasonable remuneration on the faith of which the service was originally rendered.'*

However, the success of this argument swaying the courts is unlikely, because the courts will view this as past consideration.

The second reason this will not be valid consideration is because this is an existing obligation under a contract. The authority for this is **Stilk v Myrick**[39], in which the captain of a ship promised

---

[36] (1840) 11 A & E 438
[37] (1842) 3 QB 234
[38] [1892] 1 Ch 104
[39] (1809) 2 Camp 317

his crew that, if they shared between them the work of two seamen who had deserted, the wages of the deserters would be distributed out between them. The court held that the promise was not binding because the seamen gave no new consideration: they were already contractually bound to do any extra work to complete the voyage.

We have to ask whether Roger has done any more than what he was bound to do under a previous contract with the Golden Antiques. If the answer is no, then there is no consideration. It is unlikely that the earlier work done at a discount by Roger will be valid consideration as payment for the beds. The discount was provided probably in order to secure the work.

Golden Antiques revocation

Golden Antiques sent David a fax on Wednesday evening saying that the beds were no longer available for sale. Golden Antiques received David's letter at 3.45pm on Thursday. David did not read the fax from Golden Antiques until 4.00pm on Thursday. The revocation of the offer can only take place if the offer has not been accepted. This will all hinge on whether the courts will apply the postal rule. If the Court applies the postal rule, then acceptance has taken place before revocation and there is a binding contract with David. The authority for this is **Byrne v Van Tienhoven**[40], where an offeror posted a letter on 1 October offering to sell the offeree a quantity of tinplate, then posted another letter on 8 October withdrawing the offer. The first letter reached PP on 11 October and they accepted the offer at once by telegram, following with a confirmatory letter four days later. The second letter purporting to withdraw the offer arrived on 20 October, by which time the offer had been accepted and it was too late for DD to withdraw.

Conclusion

First, the advertisement of the beds is not clear, precise and unequivocal and therefore likely to be an invitation to treat.

---

[40] (1880) LR 5 CPD 344

Second, David's email is an offer that Golden Antiques can either accept or reject. Golden Antiques have reaffirmed the price of the bed as £5,000; this is a counter offer. Third, the statement *'please advise if credit facility is available'* will be seen by the courts as a request for further information. David's acceptance by fax is incomplete; he must communicate his acceptance. Fourth, it would appear David has benefited under the postal rule and accepted the offer, and thus has a binding contract. Fifth, if the Court applies the postal rule, then acceptance has taken place before revocation and there is a binding contract with David. If Golden Antiques decides to sell to Roger, this is a breach of contract with David. Lastly, if Golden Antiques want to change their mind and does ultimately sell to David, they can because the contract with Roger may be unenforceable due to lack of consideration.

Battle of the forms essay

Question: Critically appraise whether recent judicial decisions reinforcing a resolute adherence to the rules applied to a battle of the forms scenario actually satisfies the reasonable expectations of businessmen more focused on their commercial transaction than legal doctrine?

Answer

There are two components of the essay question which require addressing: (1) what rules are applied to a battle of the forms scenario and whether they have been consistently applied by the courts; and (2) whether or not those rules satisfy the reasonable expectations of businessmen. Naturally, the answer that is to follow will address the above-mentioned matters.

For the sake of convenience and economic efficiency, commercial parties usually enter into agreements between one another via contracts containing standard terms and conditions. The problems begin to surface when both parties have differing terms and conditions and wish to contract on the terms and conditions that protect their interests the most. This gives rise to what has come to be known as the 'battle of the forms' scenario. As was expressed by His Honour Judge Havelock-Allan QC in **Sterling Hydraulics**,[41] the classic example of this type of scenario is in **Butler Machine**.[42]

This was a case where the seller offered to deliver a machine tool on its own terms and conditions, which, amongst others, contained a price variation clause entitling the seller to adjust the price in line with the prices at the date of delivery. The buyer's reply to the offer made the acceptance conditional upon its own terms and conditions. The buyer also included, with the order, a tear-off

---

[41] *Sterling Hydraulics Limited v Dichtomatik Limited* [2006] EWHC 2004 (QB) *per* Havelock-Allan QC at p. 14, *para.* [21].
[42] *Butler Machine Tool Co. Ltd. v Ex-Cell-O Corporation (England) Ltd* [1979] 1 WLR 401.

acknowledgement, which accepted the order on the "*terms and conditions thereon*". The seller returned the completed and signed acknowledgement form, but with a covering letter stating that delivery was to be "*in accordance with our revised quotation* [as contained in the offer]". A dispute arose between the parties as to whether or not the seller was entitled to the increase in costs of producing the machine. The central issue of the case thus centred on the issue of whose terms and conditions were adopted. If the buyer's terms and conditions were adopted, the seller's demand for an additional fee would be without a valid ground and was thus bound to fail.

Lord Denning MR, having expressed that the rules applied by the courts in battle of the forms cases are out of date, accepted that, in such cases, the approach to be adopted should be the "*traditional analysis of offer, counter-offer, rejection, acceptance*".[43] This analysis dictates that, where an offer is replied to with any of the terms being modified, that constitutes a counter-offer, since the acceptance must mirror the offer made that must be accepted by the other party to give rise to a valid agreement. According to Lord Denning MR, in such cases, there is a contract as soon as the last of the forms is sent and received without objection being taken to it.[44]

The battle of the forms rules, as established in *Butler Machine*, was recently considered and followed by the Court of Appeal in **Tekdata Interconnections**.[45] Longmore LJ expressed that "...*the traditional offer and acceptance analysis must be adopted unless the documents passing between the parties and their conduct show that their common intention was that some other terms were intended to prevail.*"[46] Dyson LJ (as he then was) concurred and ruled that the traditional offer and acceptance analysis is to be applied in battle of the forms cases unless the circumstances of the case leads one to conclude that the parties' intentions were to the

---

[43] Butler Machine, *supra* no 2, *per* Lord Denning MR at p. 404(F).
[44] *Ibid*, at p. 404(H).
[45] *Tekdata Interconnections Ltd v Amphenol Ltd* [2009] EWCA Civ 1209; [2009] 2 CLC 866.
[46] *Ibid, per* Longmore LJ at p. 870, *para.* [11].

contrary.[47]

This is a significant step forward. Although the traditional analysis was applied in both **Butler Machine** and **Tekdata Interconnections,** upon a careful examination of both cases, it becomes apparent that the Court of Appeal in **Tekdata Interconnection** did not completely adhere to the traditional analysis, but rather created a system whereby the traditional analysis would be considered as the default rules to be applied to a battle of the forms scenario, unless the common intention of the parties was of such a nature to warrant departure from it. Consequently, if one were to state that the recent judicial decisions reinforce a resolute adherence to the rules applied to a battle of the forms scenario, such an assertion would not accurately portray the current state of the English law as to contract formation. There seems to be a tendency by the courts to *"focus on what the parties must be taken, objectively, to have intended at the time when the contract was made"*.[48]

This, it is submitted, achieves both commercial certainty, which commercial men most desire, and flexibility required to prevent unjust and absurd results. Although **Phillip Morgan** states that the intention required will be difficult to show in a battle of forms case, unless there is a clear course of dealing between the parties and that, consequently, the common intention will be rarely found to exist, he rightfully acknowledges that, if the course of dealing between the parties were permitted to displace the default rule so easily, that would hinder commercial certainty and increase litigation.[49] Upon having read Dyson LJ (as he then was)'s judgment in **Tekdata Interconnections,** one would no doubt become aware of the degree of importance his Lordship attached to the principle of commercial certainty.

---

[47] *Ibid, per* Dyson LJ (as he then was) at p. 874, *para.* [25].
[48] *Ibid, per* Dyson LJ (as he then was) at p. 876, *para.* [30]. See also, Pill LJ at p. 876, *para.* [34].
[49] Morgan, P., '*Battle of the forms: restating the orthodox*' (2010) Cambridge Law Journal 230 at pp. 231-232.

Moving on to whether or not the above-mentioned rules satisfy the reasonable expectations of businessmen, one would have to identify what a reasonable businessman should be able to expect when a battle of the forms scenario arises. Richard J. Bragg[50] has accurately identified the considerations that are usually uppermost in a businessman's mind: economic and financial considerations. When a businessman enters into a transaction, his ultimate aim is to ensure that it has a profitable return. In the context of the present case, that equates to the avoidance of litigation and, most importantly, the acceptance by the other party of its own terms and conditions. In most cases, if not all, the validity of a disputed clause will determine whether or not a party is obliged to, for instance, make a payment to the other party or be held liable for a loss or damage sustained by the other party. Thus, the terms and conditions that the court holds as adopted and contracted upon will have a crucial effect on the businessman in question.

The most basic expectation of commercial parties would be for the courts to respect the contracts entered into and to refrain from interfering unless strictly necessary. The second, and upon which the first is partly dependent, is for the businessman to be able to ascertain with sufficient clarity the laws and rules that are to be applied when a dispute arises between the parties emanating from the contract. That would not only inform the businessman of the steps that he should take and those he should refrain from taking, but would assist him and his advisors to draft agreements that would reflect the terms upon which he wishes to engage with others.[51] It is without a doubt that those two principles are widely respected and adhered to by the English courts.[52] It is probably the most influential reason why so many agreements are entered into

---

[50] Bragg, R.J., '*The battle of the forms: another round*' (1986) Company Lawyer 209 at p. 210.

[51] *See*, Beale, H. Chitty on Contracts, 30th Ed (Sweet & Maxwell: London, 2008), Vol 1, para. 2-037; '*Drafting standard terms and conditions for the supply of services*", Practical Law Company, accessed available at http://uk.practicallaw.com/2-501 7221?q=drafting+standard+terms+and+conditions, accessed on 29 January 2012.

[52] *See, Eurico SpA v Philipp Brothers* [1987] 2 Lloyd's Rep. 215 *per* Lord Diplock at p. 218 where his Lordship said: "*A basic principle of the common law of contract ... is that parties to a contract are free to determine for themselves what primary obligations they will accept.*". See also, *Homburg Houtimport B.V. v Agrosin Private Ltd (The Starsin)* [2003] UKHL 12, [2003] 3 WLR 711 *per* Lord Bingham of Cornhill at [57].

with English law as the applicable law to the contract. Thus, English law on contract formation and the battle of the forms rules in particular, does indeed meet the reasonable expectations of businessmen. It gives them commercial certainty but, at the same time, provides the mechanism necessary for the default rules to be departed from where it is determined from the circumstances of the case that that is what they intended.

Postal rule and instantaneous communication in a modern age essay

Introduction

The postal rule can be described as arbitrary, and was created because it was felt, at the time, some rule was essential in the early 19th Century to regulate letter contracting. The principle emerged because the postal service was the only option for distance contracting. Modern technologies and inventions, namely email, makes the postal rule redundant and unfair. This essay explores the advantages, along with the criticisms, of the postal rule and whether it should and can be justified today. The Postal rule is no longer needed, because in the 21st Century, contracts can be concluded in seconds, using both instantaneous and non-instantaneous methods of communication with little or no risk of loss and delay. Therefore, it should be abandoned as an obstacle to fairness in contract law.

The Postal Rule for Acceptance

The general rule is that, once a letter of acceptance is dispatched in the post, the postal acceptance is already effectual[53]. In other words – as soon as the letter is in the control of the Post Office[54], the contracting parties are legally bound in contract. It was established back in 1818 in **Adam v Lindsell**[55], where it was

---

[53] G.H. Treitel "The Law of Contract, 12th edition (2007), para 2-028
[54] Brinkinbon Ltd v Stahag und Stahlwarenhandelsgesellschaft mbH [1983] 2 A.C. 34 at 41
[55] (1818) 1 B & Ald 681

stated that the rule was essentially a rule of convenience[56]. The postal rule is supported by saying that the offeror takes the risk (i.e. the risk of failing to receive acceptance) by initiating negotiations by post originally[57]. As a result, it does not apply to instantaneous methods of communication (i.e. telephone, telex) on the grounds that all the parties are aware of contract conclusion. Therefore, they are unlikely to face risks such as delays or failure of transmission[58].

The Postal Rule for Revocation

However, if it was reasonable to establish a specific postal rule for acceptance, consequently there may be another necessary rule concerning revocations of offers. In the case of communication by post, the general rule is that *"Dispatch of a letter or telegram of acceptance by the offeree terminates the offeror's power of revocation. Loss or delay of the letter of acceptance is immaterial and subsequent death of either party can have no effect on its formation"*[59]. In other words, the letter of revocation is effective only on delivery[60].

Reasons for the Establishment of the Postal Rule

By and large, the reason for the creation of the postal rule was to raise certainty within contractual formation[61]. Equally, in 1818 the postal service had been comparatively slow; for example, the first train from Liverpool to Manchester had made its first deliveries twenty years afterwards[62]. Therefore, the main predicament at the

---

[56] (1999) 1 EBL 5,6 , Issue 5
[57] *Ibid.*
[58] P. Fasciano "Internet Electronic Mail: A last Bastion for the Mailbox Rule" (1996 - 1997) 25 Hofstra Law Review 1542
[59] (1966) 15 ICLQ 553 at 557
[60] Established by Lindley J in Byrne & Co v Leon Van Tienhoven (1880) L.R. 5 (C.P.D.) 344, followed by Henthorn v Fraser [1892] 2 Ch. 27 and Stevenson, Jacques & Co McLean (1880) L.R. 5 (Q.B.D.) 346; Exceptions are Hebb's Case (1867) L.R. 4 Eq. 9 and Townsend's Case (1871) L.R. 13 (Eq.) 148 – in both, the letter of revocation was posted, but not delivered before the acceptance took effect. Both regard such withdrawal effective.
[61] D. Capps "You've got mail" (2003) N.L.J 906, See also Adam v Lindsell (1818) 1 B & Ald 681
[62] H. Blake, http://www.telegraph.co.uk/news/uknews/royal-mail/7814591/The-Royal-

start of the 19th Century was that the postal service had no substitute method of communication. It was Capps who suggested that, if instantaneous modes of communication were on hand, it is open to question whether an effective-on-dispatch rule would have been required[63].

There is some argument that it is easier to prove posting a letter rather than proving receipt. The reason given is that it is the offeror who chooses to use the post, so they should be at a disadvantage. Although it is true that he can elect to make the offer using telephone, the above-mentioned reason is not very compelling. It might have been the offeree who initially started the negotiations by letter[64].

Was it an arbitrary solution?

In reality, it is to some extent an illogical resolution to the dilemma of which of the participants should bear the risk where they communicate through the post[65]. At the start of the 19th Century, some rule was indispensable. This has led to Evans arguing that the reason for the relevance of the postal rule is *"no more than abdication of responsibility"*[66]. Additionally, it is noteworthy to consider the rule laid down in **Adam v Lindsell**[67] originated at a time when there was no general rule that acceptance needed to be communicated[68]. As a result, Simon Gardner argues that the Adam v Lindsell case provides limited foundation for the original postal acceptance rule[69].

There have always been problems with contract negotiations by post – even at present, letters may either be delayed or lost. Therefore, one of the contracting parties bears a risk by choosing

---

Mail-a-history-of-the-British-postal-service.html
[63] D. Capps "You've got mail" (2003) N.L.J 906
[64] L. Koffman (2001) ''The Law of Contract'' 4th edition
[65] *Ibid.*
[66] (1966) 15 ICLQ 553 at 559
[67] (1818) 1 B & Ald 681
[68] L. Koffman (2001) ''The Law of Contract''' , See also A.W.B Simpson (1975), 91 LQR 247
[69] S. Gardner (1992) 12 O.J.L.S. 2, 170-194, p. 171

the postal services for a preferred method of communication[70]. Certainly, the offeror is the party who bears that risk, under the effective-on-dispatch postal rule. However, sometimes there will be the case where the offeree starts the negotiations by letter, as mentioned in the previous section. Therefore, the postal rule needs reconsideration, bearing in mind all the technology developments in the 21st Century.

Justification of the Postal Rule

Thesiger LJ, in Household Fire and Carriage Accident Insurance Co. v Grant[71], argues that it is impossible to produce a rule that would be fair to both of the parties. However, he thinks that it is more convenient for acceptance to be effective on posting, rather than on receipt.
Another reason for justification of the postal rule is that it is logical for the offeror to bear the risk of the distance communications. He is the one who can manipulate the offer and introduce conditions. The offeree is less likely to change the conditions. Even if he does, we know that it will no longer be an acceptance of an offer, but a counter-offer[72].

The offeror can always avoid the postal rule by stipulating actual receipt or a specific way of communication, or even initiating the negotiations by instantaneous method. He can require parties to telegraph instead of using a slower method such as the postal services[73]. The offeror has the choice to set a specific time until which the acceptance should reach him. Consequently, an offer expressed to continue for a fixed time may be legally retracted before the expiration of the time limit unless previously accepted[74].

Criticism of the Postal Rule

---

[70] J. Poole, (2010) ''Contract Law'', p.67 °
[71] (1878-79) L.R. 4 Ex. D. 216, at 223
[72] J. Poole (2010) "Contract Law", 57-59
[73] Quenerduaine v Cole (1883), 32 W.R. 185
[74] "Leake's Law of Contracts" (1931) at 24

In Household Fire and Carriage Accident Insurance Co v. Grant[75], Thesiger LJ suggested that it is reasonable to treat the post office as the agent of both of the parties[76]. Evans rejected the suggestion on the basis that the post office and telegram company do not fall within the definition of agents,[77] to which acceptance may be communicated. Moreover the, Post Office, as a governmental agency for public services, works under its own regulations. In truth, both the Post Office and telegraph companies are independent contractors for the transmission of messages[78]. Hence, the Post Office is not responsible for the receipt of a letter because it is not concerned with possible misdirections[79]. Therefore, the Post Office could never be an agent, but only a carrier between the offer and the acceptance[80].

Evans explains that, under the dispatch rule, if a letter is lost it can be difficult to prove that it was correctly addressed and prepaid[81]. For example, it could be the offeree's fault that the letter did not arrive. Does that mean the offeror is the one who should suffer the consequences? Under the dispatch principle, the postal rule is one-sided and unfair for the offeror. That's why **British and American Telegraph Co v Colson**[82] proposed a compromise rule whereby, "although the letter of acceptance must be received; once received it would be retrospectively effective as from its posting". However, this proposal was rejected[83].

Another common argument for the establishment of the postal rule can be found in the dictum from **Adam v Lindsell**[84]:

> "If the [offerors] were not bound by their offer when accepted by the [offerees] till the answer was received, then the [offerees] ought not to be bound till after they

---

[75] (1878-79) L.R. 4 Ex. D. 216, at 223
[76] Stocken v Collin (1841) 151 E.R. 870; Dunlop v Higgins (1841) 7 M. & W. 515
[77] Mechem, "Agency" (2nd ed., 1914)
[78] (1966) 15 ICLQ 553 at 559
[79] Ibid.
[80] Ibid.
[81] Ibid.
[82] (1871) LR 6 (Exch) 108
[83] Harris' Case (1871-72) L.R. 7 (Ch. App.) 587
[84] (1818) 1 B & Ald 681 at 683

had received the notification that the [offerors] had received their answer and assented to it. And so it might go on ad infinitum".

However, if this reason was acceptable in the 19th Century, it is no longer relevant because of technological development and instantaneous methods of communication. Both of the parties can always check whether the offer or acceptance is successfully delivered by using telex, telephone, etc.

Postal Rule in the New Era of Technology Development

Whatever the reasons for the establishment of the postal rule in 1818, currently, the situation is completely different. As time has passed and technology has developed, the speed and range of communication has increased[85]. After the invention of the Press in the 15th Century, the Telegraph System in the 1830s, the Telephone (1876) and Telex System (1930s), the world was ready to face new technologies that would change everything. In current times, the enormous success of Google, Amazon, Facebook, E-bay, Hotmail, and Yahoo illustrates how consumer and businesses alike have embraced internet and electronic commerce in the last decade[86]. Consequently, there are many arguments that the instantaneous methods of communication and internet communications make the postal rule redundant.

E-mail communications

Unfortunately, there is still ambiguity, uncertainty, and legal arguments about e-mail contracting. The problem derives from the fact that there is no direct authority on the question of whether e-mail communication can be determined as an instantaneous or a non-instantaneous method[87]. The most common argument is that e-mail is not direct between the parties, and messages are broken up into packets that travel around internet networks[88]. Therefore,

---

[85] I. Lloyd, D. Mellor(2003) "Telecommunications Law" at p.3;
[86] Edwards, Waelde (2009) "Law and the Internet", at p.89
[87] Ibid., p.105
[88] Ibid, p.105

e-mail is a non-instantaneous method of communication and Murray[89] suggested that "postal rule should apply to e-mail acceptances, because they are neither direct, nor reliable[90] and the acceptor sending his e-mail does not know immediately whether or not the communication was successful"[91]. This is true, but there is a weakness in his judgment, for he has not considered that there is always possibility for the acceptor to check the succession of his e-mail by using telephone. Furthermore, Capps argues that the acceptor has some control over a sent e-mail in that it can often be recalled[92]. Maybe this is why Murray withdraws this interpretation later in his article, in 2005[93].

Edwards and Waelde propose one solution that would be convenient for both of the parties, suggesting that e-mail be deemed to be received when the sender receives the recipient's acknowledgment of the delivery,[94] as in **1996 UNCITRAL Model Law on E-Commerce, Art 14(3)**. Under this provision, if a data message has been made conditional on receipt, the data message is treated as though it has never been sent until the acknowledgement is received. This is why the postal rule is not such a burden if manipulated intelligently. In the US, another postal rule regulation can be seen in the **Uniform Computer Information Transactions Act 2000 (UCITA)**, where section **203(4)** states that *"if an offer in an electronic message evokes in electronic message accepting the offer, a contract is formed when an electronic acceptance is received*[95].

A frequently used moral argument for justifying the postal rule is to put the risk of delay on the party choosing the communication method[96]. However, this is no longer convincing because in the

---

[89] A.D. Murray (2000) "Entering into Contracts Electronically: The Real W.W.W..", in Edwards and Waelde (eds), "Law and the Internet: A Framework for Electronic Commerce"
[90] Clearly, the delay in e-mail communication will not be as long as the delay using postal services, but uncertainty whether a message has arrived could be just as great.
[91] Edwards, Waelde (2009) Law and the Internet, p.105
[92] D. Capps (2004) I.C.C.L.R. at 209
[93] (2005) L, Edwards (ed), "The New Legal Framework for E-Commerce in Europe"
[94] Edwards, Waelde (2009) "Law and the Internet", p.105
[95] D. Capps "You've got mail" (2003) N.L.J 906
[96] P. Todd, "E-Commerce Law" (2005) para 9.2.1

21st Century, companies have a range of communication choices to make a contract. If they would like to protect themselves from the postal rule effect, they could use instantaneous method, which will be more safe and secure. Therefore, if A makes an offer by telephone, and B sends the acceptance by e-mail that never reaches A, then A will not be legally bound and risk is put on B's decision.

Another reason why the postal rule is no longer needed is that most e-mail servers have the option to check whether an e-mail has been received and read. If the acceptor receives a failure notification, he can choose to resend it until he is certain about the successful delivery[97]. Therefore, loss and delay are no longer a problem. Even if they occur, they can be traced and corrected.

Conclusion

When the postal rule was created, it provided a reasonable answer to a genuine problem, in that the inherent delays in the principle method of communication (Postal services) led to uncertainties in contract formation. Nobody knows for certain what would have been the postal rule if established after the invention of the telegraph, telephone and telex. However, if the same rule were produced in the era of Internet and e-mail communication, it would be absolutely unreasonable. Therefore, the postal rule may have been adequate in the 19th Century. However, at the present time, it is inappropriate because of the technologies in our days, and the postal rule should be abandoned as an obstacle to fairness in contract law.

---

[97] D. Capps "You've got mail" (2003) N.L.J 906

Chapter 4 Consideration

Introduction

A contract that is not established by way of seal (by deed) needs to be backed up with some kind of consideration of value. There are, of course, some exceptions to this main general principle, as you will discover throughout this chapter. Consideration is required in all contracts and is not established by seal, only with its presence will an agreement be deemed legally enforceable.

Question and Answers

- Consideration Essay Question
- Consideration Problem Question

Consideration Essay Question

Question

Should the principle in **Williams v Roffey** *be* extended to cover the situation encountered in **re Selectmove Limited**? Give reasons for your answer.

Answer

Introduction

This essay will establish the traditional position by looking at case law such as **Stilk v Myrick**; [98]**Hartley v Ponsonby**,[99]**Pinnels case**[100] and **Foakes v Beer**.[101] Second, this paper will examine the decision in **Williams v Roffey Bros** to establish whether the law has departed from the traditional rules of consideration. Third, this paper will examine subsequent case law to see how the courts have applied the principle in **Williams v Roffey Bros**.[102] It will do this by asking the question that should the decision in **Williams v Roffey Bros** be extended to cases concerning part payment. Finally, the essay will conclude its findings.

The traditional position

In **Stilk v Myrick**, a ships' master promised his crew that the wages of the deserters would be shared out between the crew which remained. The court in these cases held that the promise to pay by the captain was not enforceable on the basis that the crew had provided any consideration. The crew was already under contract to complete the voyage. This can be praised as a good decision because it prevents unscrupulous crew members from blackmailing the ship's master into agreeing to make extra payments. This decision can be interpreted as an early attempt by the courts to protect the ship's master from the possibility of

---

[98] (1809) 2 Camp 317
[99] [1857] 26 LJ QB 322
[100] *Pinnel's Case* (1602) 5 Co Rep 117a
[101] (1884) 9 App Cas 605
[102] *Williams v Roffey Bros and Nicholls (Contractors) Limited* [1990] 1 All ER 512

economic duress.

A different approach was taken in **Hartley v Ponsonby** where, where the ships' crew had a large number of desertions. The court held that the crew should be able to recover an extra £40 pay and that this promise to pay had the necessary consideration. The court said the seamen were not obliged to do this under their existing contracts of service and were free to enter into a fresh contract. This recognised exception to **Stilk v Myrick** was approved by the court in **The Atlantic Baron**.[103]

The position in **Stilk v Myrick** seems to have also been applied to cases concerning partial payment in full satisfaction for the debt. In **Pinnel's Case**, the defendant had not provided any consideration for the plaintiffs promise not to sue on partial payment accepted. Sir Edward Coke had stated that:

"payment of a lesser sum on the day in satisfaction of a greater sum, cannot be any satisfaction for the whole, because it appears to the Judges that by no possibility, a lesser sum can be a satisfaction to the plaintiff for a greater sum."[104]

This rule was upheld and applied in the case of **Foakes v Beer**, but not without the express doubts of Lord Blackburn, who nevertheless concurred in the judgement in that case, that *"men of business ... do every day recognise and act on the ground that prompt payment of a part of their demand may be more beneficial to them than it would be to insist on their rights."*[105] Therefore, the position according to these old authorities seems to be that any attempt to vary a contract will lack consideration unless what is been received is all together new or different to the original promise.

The decision in Williams v Roffey

Roffey contracted with Williams to do some carpentry work. The

---

[103] North Ocean Shipping v Hyundai (The Atlantic Baron) [1979] QB 705
[104] *Pinnel's Case* (1602) 5 Co Rep 117a
[105] [1881–5] All ER Rep 106 at 115

price for the carpentry work was agreed at £20,000. Williams found themselves in severe financial difficulties. Roffey were concerned that they would be liable under a penalty clause in the main building contract thus they promised to pay Williams an additional sum for each flat completed on time. Roffey then declined to make any further payments. The plaintiff sued for the additional monies promised. Roffey argued that by completing on time, the Williams had done no more than he was already contractually bound to do. The court held that the promise to pay addition monies was binding. Williams had provided the necessary consideration because Roffey had obtained a 'practical benefit', namely avoiding the penalty and having avoided having to find a new sub-contractor.

Adams and Brownsword argue that the court have taken a 'robust approach' and extended the principle outside of the traditional doctrine of consideration.[106] It can be counter argued that *Roffey* is achieving a major objective. It ensures that a contracting party that makes a promise under no pressure in a commercial context will be bound by this promise, even if there is almost no consideration. The problem that this creates is that it seems to sit uneasily with the traditional common law position of consideration.

There is only one difference (that the court had the ability to deduce) between **Roffey** and **Stilk**: the practical benefit that Roffey gained in that they were prevented from paying under the penalty clause. Glidewell LJ followed **Ward v Byham**[107] where there was consideration because the mother was ordered to do more than what she was supposed to do legally. Williams was only being asked to perform their existing duty. Glidewell LJ avoided referring to **Hartley v Ponsonby** which is distinguishing the same point, that the party brought something totally different to what was in the agreement.

The fundamental issue brought out in this case is not different

---

[106] Adams and Brownsword 'Contract, consideration and the critical path' (1990) 53 MLR 540
[107] [1956] 1 WLR 496

from the doctrine of estoppel. There are two predictable difficulties. First, estoppel works on the basis that it allows acceptance of part payment of debts to be repaid as consideration for new deals. Second, estoppel works as a protection and not as an attack thus it cannot be normally used to find an action. Therefore it can be argued that if the decision in *Roffey* is a good decision, then it should apply to cases concerning part-payment of debts. [108]

Should we extend the principle in Roffey to part payment cases?

In **Re Selectmove**, a company owed tax to the Inland Revenue and offered to pay this off in instalments. The tax collector said that he would be in touch with the company if the agreement could not be reached. The IRC ordered to pay all the taxes immediately or they would take immediate actions against the company. The company tried to invoke the principle of **Williams v Roffey** that the promise they made is carrying out an obligation which is existing was supporting the consideration for the deal to pay the debts in parts. The Court of Appeal differentiated **Williams v Roffey** that it contained the precedent of services and goods not debt payments. However, the distinction can be criticised as artificial and it can be suggested that there is no logical reason why the principle should not be extended to apply equally to both types of cases. The precedent that the court followed was **Foakes v Beer** and held that the IRC was not under any agreement binding them to accept part-payments. While the decision in this case shows that it conflicts with the ratio decidendi in **Williams v Roffey**, it could be obvious that the fundamental principle of paying the debts in parts is still unaffected.

It can be argued that extending the principle of **Roffey** to part-payment of debts would have severe consequence for creditors in insolvency. If a business goes into liquidation then the administrator may seek to recover part-payment of debts to discharge the larger debt in full and final settlement. This is

---

[108] See for example the discussion in Trietel, G.H. *Some Landmarks of 20th Century Contract Law*, Oxford University Press, Oxford, 2002, pp38-40,

damaging to creditors and could as a result have harmful effect on the economy as it shifts the risk of business onto the creditor.

The Court of Appeal could have extended **Roffey** to part-payment of debts in **Selectmove**. However, it must be pointed out that the court's decision not to do so and follow **Foakes v Beer** was necessary. The Court of Appeal has no power to overrule **Foakes v Beer** as it was a decision of the House of Lords. More recently in **South Caribbean Trading Ltd ('SCT') v Trafigura Beeher BV** [109]Colman J cast doubt on the decision in **Williams v Roffey Bros**. He noted that the decision was inconsistent with the long-standing rule that consideration must move from the promisee.[110] He further noted that the House of Lords had yet to declare that **Williams v Roffey Bros** was wrongly decided.

Conclusion

This paper has presented the traditional position as stated in **Stilk v Myrick** and recognised that the principle of **Roffey** seems to be an exception to that. It appears the courts have extended the principle to meet the requirements of justice in **Roffey**. It should not be seen as an overriding principle of law but a rule which courts have decided not to extend in **Re Selectmove.** Further, as this matter seems to also effect the law of insolvency (which is based on who gets paid what on a winding up) the proper body to change the law in this case is Parliament.

---

[109] [2004] EWHC 2676
[110] [2004] EWHC 2676 (paras.106–09 of the judgment)

Consideration Problem Question

Question

Debra hired Simon, a builder, to construct a single storey extension on the back of her house. Simon promised to complete the work by 30th December for £10,000. Debra agreed and paid Simon a deposit of £3,000.

Simon commenced the work on time but due to his poor health and a failure to supervise his workers, the job fell significantly behind schedule. Debra, who was hoping to throw a New Year's Eve party in the new extension, was eager to ensure that the work would be completed on time. She promised Simon an extra £2,000 provided that he meets the original 30th December deadline. Simon agreed.

The work was completed on December 29th and Simon sent Debra an invoice for £9,000. Debra told Simon that she was in financial difficulties and could only pay £7,000. Simon needed this money in order to buy materials for his next job and so he felt that he had no alternative but to accept this amount in full and final settlement.

Simon has recently read that Debra has won £1m on the National Lottery.

Advise Simon whether he is entitled to demand the extra £2,000 promised by Debra.

Answer

Introduction

This paper advises Simon on his position in relation to his agreement with Debra. The paper examines the difficulties faced by Simon in arguing that he is in fact entitled to the additional £2,000 promised by Debra. In particular, this paper will address the issue of consideration and the possible implications of promissory estoppel and economic duress.

Consideration for the variation

It is first necessary to address whether the variation of the terms in this case is a binding variation of the contract. This variation will only be enforceable where it satisfies the formal requirements governing the formation of contract, and therefore consideration must be present. In the case of **Currie v Misa**, Lush J referred to consideration as *'[...] some right, interest, profit or benefit accruing to one party, or some forbearance, detriment, loss or responsibility, given, suffered or undertaken by the other'*.

On the facts of this case, it does not appear that there has been any further consideration to support the variation of the agreement. Whilst it is clear that Simon will receive the further benefit of the additional £2,000, it is more difficult to establish the benefit received by Debra. This suggests that the variation is not mutually beneficial and therefore not enforceable. It may however be possible to argue that Debra will gain the benefit of having the new extension built in time for her New Year's Eve party which may be a practical benefit.

It is important to consider the case law in this area in determining whether Simon can argue that Debra received a practical benefit, which amounted to consideration. In **Stilk v Myrick**, after failing to find replacements, the captain promised his crew that the wages of the deserters would be shared out between them if they fulfilled the duties of the missing crewmen as well as their own. The court held that the promise was not binding, as the crew had not given consideration in respect of the promise. Applying this to the facts of our case, it seems unlikely that Simon would recover the additional £2,000. Debra could argue that Simon merely discharged their pre-existing duty, and therefore no additional benefit was conferred on them. As a result, Debra may argue consideration was not present and the variation was therefore not binding on them.

The exception to this principle was established in **Hartley v Ponsonby** where a ship's crew had been seriously depleted by a number of desertions. The captain promised the remaining crew members £40 extra pay if they would complete the voyage. It was held by the court that this promise was binding. The crew had provided valid consideration because it was dangerous to sail so undermanned. The seamen were not obliged to do this under their contracts of service and were; therefore, free to enter into a fresh contract, which would include the extra remuneration, for the remaining part of the voyage.

This exception was developed even further in **Williams v Roffey Bros. & Nicholls (Contractors) Ltd**. Here a building contractor was refurbishing a block of twenty-seven flats. The building contractor subcontracted with the plaintiff, who undertook to provide certain carpentry work for the price of £20,000. The plaintiff later found himself in severe financial difficulties despite having received £16,200. The building contractor promised to pay the plaintiff an additional sum for each flat completed on time, as they were concerned that they would be liable under a penalty clause and realized that the contract was under-priced. The plaintiff completed eight further flats and the building contractor paid a further £1,500, but would not pay any additional monies. In a similar way to **Stilk v Myrick**, the building contractors argued that the plaintiff had merely done what he was already bound to do. Unlike **Stilk v Myrick** however, the court held that the building contractor received certain practical benefits including not losing out on money under the penalty clause and the cost and inconvenience of finding an alternative contractor.

On the basis of this decision, it may therefore be a valid argument that the benefit received by Debra in having the extension built before the 30th December deadline was a practical benefit. However, it is not clear that the principles in **Williams v Roffey** would extend this far. Whilst it is not addressed in the facts of our case, it may be that Debra wants no sign of building work if she is having guest over, which would not be there if the extension is built. This would certainly be a situation covered by the concept of practical benefit, although more details would be required to determine whether such practical benefits did arise.

Economic duress

If consideration can be established, the second issue to consider is economic duress. In particular, it is necessary to determine whether Simon's behaviour could be characterized as either illegitimate commercial pressure, which would render the contract voidable, or merely 'the rough and tumble of normal commercial bargaining', which would potentially allow Simon to recover the £2,000. This appears to be relevant as Debra states that she reluctantly agreed to the additional monies, as it needed to have the extension built before the 30th December deadline. The most recent definition of economic duress can be found in **DSND Subsea Ltd v Petroleum Geo-Services ASA**, in which Dyson J stated that:

> '[...] there must be pressure, (a) whose practical effect is that there is compulsion on, or lack of practical choice for, the victim, (b) which is illegitimate, and (c) which is a significant case inducing the claimant to enter into the contract.'

It may be arguable that the compulsion or lack of practical choice for the victim was not illegitimate, but was instead the exertion of pressure to be expected in a normal commercial environment. It is necessary to gain further information to determine whether this is a possible argument. Dyson J set out a number of principles to determine whether the pressure was illegitimate. In particular, it would be important for Simon to demonstrate that they were acting in good faith, that Debra had a realistic alternative but to submit to the pressure and that Debra did not protest to the variation. Whilst the threatened breach of the contract by Simon would suggest illegitimate compulsion, evidence of the other factors discussed could still lead to a finding in favour of Simon.

Promissory estoppel

The next issue to be examined is the application of promissory estoppel. The doctrine of promissory estoppel applies where *"a promise was made which was intended to create legal relations and which, to the knowledge of the person making the promise, was going to be acted on by the person to whom it was made and which was in fact so acted on"*. It is clear in this definition that the doctrine of promissory estoppel may therefore apply in our case. It can be argued that Debra made an unequivocal promise, which was intended to affect the legal relationship between the parties. It is also arguable that Debra knew that the promise was going to be acted on, as Simon made it clear he would finish before the 30th December deadline on the basis of Debra' promise. Finally, Simon then relied upon this promise.

There are two limitations to the doctrine of promissory estoppel however. First, it must inequitable for the promisor to go back on the promise (**D & C Builders v Rees**). It is arguable that it is unfair for Debra to go back on their agreement to pay the additional £2,000 to Simon. However, because she has won the lottery it would seem to be inequitable for her to go back on her word considering she is no longer in financial trouble.

Second, and more problematic, is that promissory estoppel cannot be used as a separate cause of action. This may provide difficulties for Simon, as they will want to make a claim to recover the £2,000. There may be two ways in which this problem can be addressed. First, Simon could make a claim based on Debra' promise and then only rely on promissory estoppel as a defence to Debra's argument that the terms of the original contract were still binding. Second, Simon could argue that, in not relying on promissory estoppel, they provided good consideration for the promise to pay the extra £2,000. However, promissory estoppel is merely suspensory and therefore it is possible that Debra could bring the promissory estoppel to an end by giving reasonable notice. It is not clear what reasonable notice would be, although the short length of the contract may mean that little notice would be required.

Conclusion

In conclusion, it is possible that Simon will be able to recover the £2,000 on the basis that consideration was present. Whilst this argument appears weak, Simon may be able to rely upon **Williams v Roffey** in establishing consideration, which appears to be their strongest argument. The next issue to overcome is economic duress. It seems arguable that economic duress was not present in our case, although further information is necessary to determine the strength of this argument. The doctrine of promissory estoppel may also be useful in establishing Simon's claim for the additional monies, although again limitations do exist. Whilst it is possible that Simon could therefore recover the monies on the basis of these arguments, it is by no means certain and further information is necessary before it is possible to determine the likelihood of recovery.

Chapter 5   Duress and Economic Duress

Introduction

One of the defining mechanisms in the Law of Contract is that parties can only establish contracts of their own free will and enter into them of their own free will. As a result, any party that has been influenced or forced into entering an agreement could evade the obligations of that contract by using the principle of duress. This largely rests, however, on the kinds of influences and pressures that the affected party is subjected to.

Question and Answers

- **Duress Essay Question**

Duress Essay Question

Question

"The doctrine of duress is without rational foundation and unjustifiably violates the basic principle of freedom of contract." Critically discuss.

Answer

Introduction

This paper will discuss the proposition that the doctrine of duress and its justification. It will examine the doctrine and critically discuss if it violates and sit uncomfortably with the principle of freedom of contact. In order to do this, the paper will discuss the basic principle of freedom of contract. Second it will discuss what duress is? Third it will discuss the tests of economic duress laid down by Dyson J in **DSND** and the application of the test in *Carillion*. Fourth this paper will examine the jurisprudence of economic duress. Fifth this paper will argue restitution is a better remedy than duress. Last this paper will conclude.

The principle of freedom of contract

In the nineteenth century the common Law of Contract saw a huge growth where due to significant commercial and industrial development, witnessed numerous contract disputes being brought to the courts. A superseding rule of freedom of contract followed which outlined that parties who were of full capacity should have full freedom to make any terms as long as they were legal. The result of this resulted in the rule of freedom of contract was the rule of sanctity of contract, where contracts that were willingly entered into by individuals that were of rational capacity should be enforced by the courts. In **Printing and Numerical Registering Co v Sampson**,[111] Sir George Jessel stated:

> "...*men of full age and competent understanding shall have the*

---

[111] (1875) 19 Eq 462

utmost liberty in contracting, and that their contracts, when entered into freely and voluntarily, shall be held sacred and shall be enforced by Courts of Justice."

This statement indicates that where a person is reasonable and capable then they have a choice over how they both start and complete their contracts. Nevertheless, towards the latter of the nineteenth and during the twentieth century, there was a rise in numbers of Acts of Parliament that focused on the rule of freedom of contract. This was due to it becoming more frequently recognised that the do it yourself application in regards to the rule of freedom of contract on more occasions resulted in injustice. Freedom of Contract therefore could be abused as a result of gross inequality of bargaining power between both large companies and consumers or employees; an example of this is ecominic duress or template agreements.

Potential parties to contracts should enter the market using their own thinking to ensure that they decide which bargains will work in their favour and stick to them. This freedom authorises parties to openly choose others as consensual contractual partners. Parties need to be free to express and choose their own individual terms due to each contract needing to be unique, based on the differences of people characters and what they want to expect to see from their contracts and how it can benefit them. Nevertheless the growth of both private and public sector large corporate enterprises made it almost impossible for the fragile party to exercise freedom, this is due to the pressure on for forming agreements with larger companies. Hence a party could be apprehended to the will of these more economically powerful contracting parties rather than practising their rights to an equal tender.

What is duress?

Judges have a tendency not into get involved with contracts.[112] On the other hand parties that are entering contracts need to be able to preserve assurance in terms that the contract will be adhered to

---

[112] Atiyah " Economic Duress and the ' Overborne Will" ' (1982) 98 L.Q.R. 197

which will ensure that no other party will be exploited.[113] An example of where intervention by the court is seen in duress.[114] Economic duress was known under the common law in 1976 as an acceptable ground to avoid an agreement. The first case where the doctrine arose was **Occidental Worldwide Investment Corp v Skibs**.[115] In this case it was insisted by charters of two ships that the cost to rent a ship must be reduced due to the fall in market rates by intimidating the owners about their assets and stated that unless costs were to be reduced then they would go into bankruptcy. The charterers were aware that if the ships were returned then given the slump they would face monetary difficulty and therefore would be unable to find substitute charterers. The result of this was that the threats that were made were false and deceitful meaning that owners were able to escape the renegotiated terms. Nevertheless Kerr J. acknowledged that in principle economic duress can be used to void the agreement.

In **North Ocean Shipping Ltd v Hyundai Corporation Co**, shipbuilders without any legal explanation threatened to dismiss the contract unless an increase of 10 per cent was settled by the plaintiff. The ship owners agreed to additional payment due to dreading a loss in the charter if the ship was not supplied on time. Mocatta J detailed: *"compulsion may take the form of 'economic duress' if necessary facts are proved. A threat to break a contract may amount to such 'economic duress'".* Similarly, Lord Scarman in **Pao On v Lau Yiu Long**[116] concluded: *"there is nothing contrary to principle to recognising economic duress as a factor which may render a contract voidable".*[117]

The tests of economic duress

In a number of small cases Economic duress has been applied.[118] Two cases important cases are **DSND Subsea v. Petroleum Geo-**

---

[113] Chitty on Contracts (29th ed., Sweet & Maxwell, London, 2004)
[114] *Barton v Armstrong* [1976] AC 104
[115] [1976] 1 Lloyd's Rep. 293
[116] [1980] A.C. 614
[117] [1980] A.C. 614 at 636
[118] *Atlas Express Ltd v Kafco Ltd* [1989] Q.B. 333

Services[119] and *Carillion Construction Ltd v Felix (UK) Ltd.*[120] Dyson J was the judge who decided both of these cases. Ecominic duress was discovered in the latter case but was not in *DSND*. According to Dyson J in the *DSND*:

> *"The ingredients of actionable duress are that there must be pressure, (a) whose practical effect is that there is compulsion on, or a lack of practical choice, for the victim, (b) which is illegitimate, and (c) which is a significant cause inducing the claimant to enter into the contract ... In determining whether there has been illegitimate pressure, the court takes into account a range of factors. These include whether there has been an actual or threatened breach of contract; whether the person allegedly exerting the pressure has acted in good or bad faith; whether the victim protested at the time; and whether he affirmed and sought to rely on the contract. These are all relevant factors".*

Dyson J ended this test by placing a proviso, which has famously made economic duress very hard to argue:

> *"Illegitimate pressure must be distinguished from the rough and tumble of the pressures of normal commercial bargaining."*

DSND

DSND were hired by Petroleum Geo-Services (PGS) to work under the sea as part of developing oil rig sites and drilling platforms in the North Sea. The original contract had been altered by succeeding agreements. These had changed the payment terms for aspects of the work. Having made these agreements, PGS wanted to have them struck down in court because of economic duress. The court held that PGS could have pursued alternative kinds of action that would have clearly allowed for them to avoid this situation, therefore they could not claim for duress. Dyson J

---
[119] [2000] BLR 531
[120] [2001] B.L.R. 1

relating the test to the evidence, said:

> " [a] suspension of the work on the RTIAS pending resolution of the insurance/indemnity question, even if it was a breach of contract, and even if it amounted to pressure, did not amount to illegitimate pressure. It was reasonable behaviour by a contractor acting bona fide in a very difficult situation".[121]

Carillion

In **Carillion**, the test for economic duress was awarded. Carillion was the core contractor asked to build an office building. Carillion delegated the supply, manufacture and design of the cladding to Felix. If the office was to be completed late then a charge of £75,000 per week would have to be made by Carillion to the developer for liquidated ascertained damages. Knowing Felix had fallen behind with completion, it asserted that Carillion sign the contract in relation to the monetary account which at the time was being disputed, prior to Felix completing the delivery of the cladding. Dyson J referred to his test for economic duress laid down in *DSND* and applied it to the facts of **Carillion.** Unless an agreement was made Felix threatened not to complete any more deliveries, which would result in a breach of contract.

Carillion needed to complete the job and were unable to do so without the cladding from Felix. The cladding was an important part of the task and Carillion were frantic for the cladding to be completed. Unless the cladding was to be completed the other trades would be unable to begin their tasks and would result in the whole project being delayed. Felix provided bespoke cladding and there were no other options for Carillion. There was no opportunity for settlement as it would have still taken a further six weeks to gain a decision and there were major complications in gaining a mandatory injunction. Felix had no power when asking for their final account to be paid before the completion of work nor did Felix have the right to stop deliveries until payment was made as this was not stated in the contract. In addition to this, Felix

---

[121] [2000] B.L.R. 530 at 546

was claiming in excess of what they were contractually entitled to were mindful that Carillion had no other substitute and therefore would have no other option but to concede to their demands for the sum. Based on the facts Carillion would have never entered the commercial settlement agreement if Felix had threatened not to deliver the cladding. Additionally, Carillion indicated in their correspondence at the *"extreme displeasure at being required to enter into such an agreement"*.

The jurisprudence of economic duress

Due to the broad nature of Dyson J's test judges are now not willing to break the parties' bargain. The main ideology operating in this area seemed to be market individualism.[122] This involved two principles one being the market philosophy and the other individualistic philosophy. Market philosophy views the operation of the law of contract as the result of competitive exchange. Individualism is about *"freedom of contract"* and *"sanctity of contract"*. It is fundamental to ensure that individuals have full licence in making the terms of their agreements, but also to ensure that parties are held to their contracts. Indications of this can be seen in *Pao On,* where Lord Scarman stated:

> *"Where businessmen are negotiating at arm's length it is unnecessary for the achievement of justice, and unhelpful in the development of the law to invoke such a rule of public policy. It would also create unacceptable anomaly. It is unnecessary because justice requires that men, who have negotiated at arm's length, be held to their bargains, unless it can be shown that their consent was vitiated by fraud, mistake or duress".*[123]

In addition, in **CTN Cash and Carry v Gallagher Ltd**,[124] Steyn L.J. was extremely cautious when arguing out the significance of commercial certainty:

---

[122] J. N. Adams and R. Brownsword, *Understanding Contract Law* (4th ed., Sweet & Maxwell, London, 2004)
[123] [1980] A.C. 614 at 634
[124] [1994] 4 All E.R. 714 at 719

"[allowing lawful act duress] *would introduce a substantial and undesirable element of uncertainty in the commercial bargaining process. Moreover it will often enable bona fide settled accounts to be reopened when parties to commercial dealings fall out".*

Steyn L.J. was unhappy about the courts delving to see if the contracts where socially or morally unacceptable. Part of market individualism contains reducing or completely eradicating any moral or legal factors that as a result could lead to uncertainty. Freedom of contract theory can explain the decisions in ***Atlas Express Ltd v Kafco*** **and** ***North Ocean Shipping***. It is argued whilst the difference between economic duress and legitimate commercial pressure may in some ways be unclear; the courts will usually find economic duress where the facts are captivating.[125] An example of this would be in *Atlas*, where the plaintiff carriers under-priced a contract where they were to transport basket-ware to numerous retail outlets which commanded that costs should be modified upwards. The plaintiffs further developed a new agreement and gave drivers strict directions stating that unless the defendants signed the agreement they were to drive away with the defendant's goods. The defendants had no other choice but to sign this agreement as it was so close to Christmas and as a result they could not make any further substitute provisions nor could they let down retail outlets.

It is argued duress is fact specific. If facts do not appear captivating then as a result may not fall within the test for economic duress. It is said that decisions of the court based upon market-individualism show us the test of economic duress is hard to satisfy for those involved in the rough and tumble of commercial business, but who have in turn been unfairly exploited. It is advised that's victims should look elsewhere for remedy. The remedy of restitution is not dependent on making contracts void and so the *"freedom of contract"* theory should not present a hurdle.

Restitution to the rescue

---

[125] D. Tan, " Constructing a Doctrine of Economic Duress" (2002) 18 Const. L.J. 87

The law of restitution dictates that a claimant is able to recover a benefit rather than receive compensation for breach of contract. Lord Wright stated in 1943 that:

"It is clear that any civilised system of law is bound to provide remedies for cases of what has been called unjust enrichment or unjust benefit, that is, to prevent a man from retaining the money of, or some benefit derived from, another which it is against conscience that he should keep".[126]

Restitutionary remedies are widely different from remedies in the law of both contract and tort and have been recognised under English law by the House of Lords.[127] It is said in the present situation that victims should, rather than seeking a rescission should seek restitution.[128] In the present case, *"unjust enrichment"* is the main theory based for restitution required by the victim. Unfair restitutionary remedies are only accessible where the defendant has been unfairly enriched at the cost of the victim.[129] This is the presumption upon which the victim is looking for redress because the obstacle of avoiding the contract is impossible to overcome or deal with successfully.[130] Lord Hoffmann said that the ingredients of restitution are:

"First, whether the defendant would be enriched at the plaintiff's expense; secondly, whether such enrichment would be unjust; and thirdly, whether there are nevertheless reasons of policy for denying a remedy".[131]

Conclusion

In conclusion, it is shown that the test for economic duress is broad ranging. The idea of Freedom of Contract puts courts under pressure therefore leaving them unwilling to get involved with

---

[126] *Fibrosa Spolka Akcyjna v Fairbairn Lawson Combe Barbour* [1943] A.C. 32 at 61
[127] *Lipkin Gorman Ltd v Karpnale Ltd* [1991] 2 A.C. 548
[128] *B&S Contracts v Victor Green Publications* [1984] I.C.R. 419
[129] R. Halson, " Opportunism, Economic Duress and Contractual Modifications" (1991) 107 L.Q.R. 649-678
[130] G. Virgo, The Principles of the Law of Restitution (Clarendon Press, Oxford, 1999).
[131] *Banque Financière de la Cité v Parc (Battersea) Ltd* [1999] 1 A.C. 221 at 234 per Lord Hoffmann

commercial contracts. Only when accurate circumstances are presented then there is a possibility that they may thrive to avoid the contract, although affirmation still remains. It may be more useful for victims to instead depend on restitution. There are categories of unfair enrichment that may be held open. It may be easier to bring an action in unjust enrichment than it is to satisfy the requirements of duress. The reason behind this is that the court is happy to set aside market-individualism theory in protecting unjust enrichment. The court justifies this because it is not voiding a contract rather neutralising opportunistic commercial behaviour. Restitution seems to be the way to go.

Chapter 6 Promissory Estoppel and Waivers

Question and Answer

1. Promissory Estoppel Essay

Promissory Estoppel Essay

Question

"A promise to accept a smaller sum [in satisfaction of a greater debt], if acted upon, is binding notwithstanding the absence of consideration" Per Denning J in ***Central London Property Trust Ltd v High Trees House Ltd*** [1947] KB 130.

Explain the statement with reference to consideration and the doctrine of promissory estoppel. To what extent does this statement represent an accurate view of the law?

Answer

Introduction

This paper will discuss that promise to accept smaller amount of money in satisfaction of a greater debt is not enforceable and the concept of promissory estoppel will be discussed.

Promise to accept smaller amount of money

In **Pinnel's Case** the defendant had not provided any consideration for the plaintiff's promise not to sue on partial payment accepted. Sir Edward Coke had stated that:

> *"payment of a lesser sum on the day in satisfaction of a greater, cannot be any satisfaction for the whole, because it appears to the Judges that by no possibility, a lesser sum can be a satisfaction to the plaintiff for a greater sum."*[132]

This rule was upheld and applied in the case of *Foakes v Beer*, but not without the express doubts of Lord Blackburn, who nevertheless concurred in the judgement in that case, that *"men of business ... do every day recognise and act on the ground that prompt payment of a part of their demand may be more beneficial*

---

[132] *Pinnel's Case* (1602) 5 Co Rep 117a

to them than it would be to insist on their rights. "[133]Therefore, the position according to these old authorities seems to be that any attempt to vary a contract (and promise to accept a smaller sum [in satisfaction of a greater debt]), will lack consideration unless what is been received is all together new or different to the original promise.

Where payment of a lesser sum discharges an obligation to pay a greater sum

The rule as stated above is only applicable if the promise of the creditor to accept a lesser sum is unsupported by fresh consideration from the promisee. However, if, at the creditor's request, some new element is introduced, such as payment at a different place, or at a different time, compliance with this request will amount to consideration for the waiver. This concept was acknowledged in **Pinnel's Case** itself.

Pinnel's Case (1602): here Pinnel sued Cole in debt for £8 10s due on a bond on 11 November 1600. Cole's defence was that, at Pinnel's request, he had paid him £5 2s 6d on 1 October and that Pinnel had accepted this payment in full satisfaction of the original debt. Judgment was given for the plaintiff on a point of pleading but the court made it clear that, had it not been for a technical flaw, they would have found for the defendant on the ground that the part payment had been made on an earlier date than that stipulated in the bond. Early payment was a 'new element' which clearly would benefit the creditor and would therefore amount to consideration for the promise to accept a lesser sum.

It is also clear from the case itself that the tender of a different chattel at the request of the creditor could amount to fresh consideration. The chattel may totally replace the money owed or may be tendered along with a partial payment. Consistent with the law as already stated, the court will not enquire as to whether the chattel is of an equivalent monetary value to the debt as if there is sufficient consideration it matters not whether it is adequate. It is stated in the case that 'a hawk, a horse, or a robe may clear the

---

133 [1881–5] All ER Rep 106 at 115

debt but an offer of 19s 6d in the £1 on the due date at the appointed place will not suffice'.

This view was affirmed in **Sibree v Tripp** (1846) 15 M & W 23, where Baron Alderson said: *'It is undoubtedly true that payment of a portion of a liquidated demand, in the same manner as the whole liquidated demand ought to be paid, is payment only in part; because it is not one bargain, but two; namely payment of part and an agreement, without consideration, to give up the residue . . . But if you substitute a piece of paper or a stick of sealing wax, it is different, and the bargain may be carried out in its full integrity. A man may give, in satisfaction of a debt of £100, a horse of the value of £5, but not £5. Again, if the time or place of payment be different, the one sum may be in satisfaction of the other.'*

In the case itself it was argued that the tender of a promissory note was a sufficient novelty to constitute consideration for the creditor's promise to accept a lesser sum. This was based on the argument that, by accepting the peculiar obligation inherent in a negotiable security, the debtor would be doing something which he was not already bound to do. Baron Alderson said, *'if for money you give a negotiable security, you pay it in a different way. The security may be worth more or less; it is of uncertain value. That is a case falling within the rule of law as enunciated.'*

An attempt to draw on this decision was made in **D & C Builders v Rees** [1966] 2 QB 617 where it was suggested that part payment by cheque (a negotiable instrument) was a sufficiently new element to exonerate the partly paid debt. The plaintiffs here had done some building work for the defendants and payment of £482 was still outstanding 6 months after payment had first been demanded. The defendant's wife (acting on his behalf) offered the plaintiffs £300 in full and final settlement. The plaintiff's reluctantly accepted the cheque marked, 'in completion of account' because they were in severe financial difficulties; a fact known to the defendant's wife. The plaintiffs then brought the action to recover the balance. Lord Selbourne distinguished the **Sibtree** case. He said that in no way in 1965 could it be better to have a cheque for a lesser amount than to have the whole amount in cash. The court also took into account the element of economic duress here and said that the defendants have used their knowledge of the plaintiffs' financial difficulties in order to intimidate them. There was some suggestion at the time that this decision heralded the death knell for the rule in *Pinnel* and that a watchful eye on economic duress would negate the need for such a rule. To date, this has not proved to be the case: **Re Selectmove** (1995). Part payment of a debt at a different place can amount to valuable consideration but only if the payment at the different place confers a benefit on the creditor.

Promissory Estoppel

Promissory estoppel can operate as an equitable exception to the general rule that part payment of a debt without fresh consideration does not discharge the debt obligation. **Central London Property Trust Ltd. v High Trees House Ltd**: in September 1939 the plaintiffs leased a block of flats to the defendants, who planned to lease out the individual flats. When the Second World War broke out the defendants had difficulty in leasing all of the flats and so the landlord agreed in 1940 to accept just half of the ground rent stipulated in the lease. This arrangement continued until 1945 by which time all the flats were fully let and the plaintiffs sought to return to the terms of the original agreement. The plaintiff brought an action against the defendant claiming the full original rent both for the future and the last two quarters of 1945. Denning J held that the action should succeed. The parties intended the reduction of the rent to be a temporary measure while the flats could not be fully let. The flats were fully let early in 1945 and therefore Denning held that the plaintiffs should be able to recover the full rent from the last two quarters of 1945 onwards. Denning J expressed the view, *obiter*, that the plaintiffs would not have been able to recover the rent for the 1940 – 1945 period even though there was no consideration for the promise to accept reduced rent. The reason for this was that he thought that there was a general equitable principle whereby:

'*A promise intended to be binding, intended to be acted on and in fact acted on, is binding so far as its terms properly apply.'*

The decision is controversial since it appears to conflict with **Foakes v Beer** (1884) 9 App Cas 605. The case of **Foakes v Beer** established that part payment of a debt could never be good consideration for satisfaction of the whole of the debt. However, despite the adoption of the doctrine by the courts, there has been acute judicial keenness to constrain it within very strict parameters, and these will now be considered. One of the ways the courts have tried to get around this problem is by adding the requirement that it must be Inequitable for the promisor to go back on his promise for the promise to raise promissory estoppel.

The use of promissory estoppel, as an equitable doctrine, and is at the discretion of the courts. Even if all the other elements of the doctrine are made out, it may still not be applied because it would be inequitable in the circumstances to do so. This point is well illustrated by **D & C Builders v Rees** [1965] 3 All ER 837 where the builders agreed to accept a cheque for the sum of £300 in full and final settlement of a debt of £482. Lord Denning said that because this promise had been extracted from the plaintiff creditors by intimidation on the part of the debtor, the debtor could not rely on the doctrine of promissory estoppel, since *he who seeks equity must do equity.* Thus although in **D & C,** A acted upon a promise to accept a smaller sum and **Rees** the courts prevented them from availing from the argument of promissory estoppel, as an equitable doctrine on the basis they had acted in a unequitable way.

Chapter 7 Intention to Create Legal Relations

Introduction

A legally binding contract can only exist when the contracting parties intend to form a legal relationship. Depending upon the relationship, one may assume that the parties either intended or did not intend to create legal relations. However, the intention to create legal relations can exist or not exist in a variety of circumstances; persons with a social or domestic relationship may indeed intend to create legal relations, while persons outside of these relationships may not. Contracts may fall into the category of domestic and social agreements, which are most likely to be considered without intention to create legal relations, or commercial agreements, which will typically possess intention to create legal relations.

Question and Answers

- Problem Question Intention to Create Legal Relations

Problem Question Intention to Create Legal Relations

Question

Michael has made the following promises:

a. He promises to sell his 3 year old BMW car to Chithra for £100.00 as he has recently won a new expensive car in a competition

b. On returning from holiday he promises Rachel, his daughter, £50.00 as she had cleaned his house for him whilst he was away

c. He has engaged Daniel to build a conservatory, at an agreed price of £15,500, the work to be completed in 6 months, in time for his wife's birthday party. After 3 months, it became apparent to Daniel that he would not be able to complete the job for the agreed price. He tells Michael that he needs another £2000, otherwise he will quit. Mindful of not wanting to upset the birthday plans, Michael promises to pay the extra £2000. Michael has now changed his mind about the extra payment.

You are required to advise Michael:

The rules relating to the requirement of consideration and intention to create legal relations in the law of contract and If he can be required by the law of contract to fulfil these promises.

Answer

Introduction

This paper will be advising Michael on whether he has intended to create legal obligations through promises he has made, and whether he is required to fulfil these promises under the requirement of consideration, also considering his intentions to be legally bound. This paper will cover the issues determining whether Michael; promising to sell his three-year old BMW to Chithra for £100.00, promising his daughter Rachel £50.00 as she had cleaned his house for him while he was away. Finally this advice will discuss whether Michael is legally obligated to pay Daniel an extra £2000 for building his conservatory. The advice will specifically examine consideration, economic duress and promissory estoppel. Lastly this advice will conclude its findings.

Relevance of consideration

In all of the different scenarios, the persons will have enforceable contracts, only if they can show consideration was provided by them for the promises made. It is first necessary to address the fact that consideration must be present within an agreement to make it a legally enforceable contract. In the case of **Currie v Misa**[134], Lush J referred to consideration as *"some right, interest, profit or benefit accruing to one party, or some forbearance, detriment, loss or responsibility, given, suffered or undertaken by the other"*.[135]

Michael's promise to sell the BMW

Michael promised to sell his 3 year old BMW car to Chithra for £100.00 as he won a new expensive car. The question is: was there sufficient consideration and can Chithra bring an action against Michael for this promise? Consideration must be sufficient. It can range from some form of payment to other interests of value under the law. Consideration must also be 'adequate', in terms of a bargain being made, although it is not imperative. Sufficiency remains of prime importance when forming a contract. A case authority establishing this principle is **Thomas v Thomas**,[136] where the court held that as long as there is valid consideration under the authority of **Currie v Misa**[137] then the agreement has some benefit or detriment to the parties. Furthermore in **Chappel v Nestle**,[138] the courts stated the chocolate wrappers purported

---
[134] [1875] LR 10 Ex 153, 162
[135] Currie v Misa [1875] LR 10 Ex 153, 162
[136] (1842) 2 Q.B. 851
[137] ibid
[138] [1960] A.C. 87

consideration. It was held that the offer Nestle made for the exchange of chocolate wrappers provided that they were of some value. In advice to Michael, if Michael promised to sell his 3 year old BMW to Chithra for £100, this may not be the market value of the car. However, the £100 will still be deemed to be of some value, hence valid consideration, making the promise to sell the car enforceable by Chithra.

Relevance of Intention to create legal obligations

A vital component in the formation of contract is the intention to create legal relations. If there is no clear intention to be legally bound by the parties then no contract has been formed. The courts pursue the expressed or assumed, objective intentions, of both persons in the contract. In **Rose and Frank Co. v Crompton Bros.**[139] Atkin LJ said, in the Court of Appeal, that: *"To create a contract there must be a common intention of the parties to enter into legal obligations, mutually communicated expressly or impliedly."* Moreover in the same case, Scrutton LJ said:

> *"Now it is quite possible for parties to come to an agreement by accepting a proposal with the result that the agreement does not give rise to legal relations. The reason for this is that the parties do not intend that their agreement shall give rise to legal relations. This intention may be implied from the subject matter of the agreement, but it may also be expressed by the parties. In social and family relations such an intention is readily implied, while in business matters, the opposite result would ordinarily follow".*

Intention to create legal obligations

Michael promised to sell his 3 year old BMW car to Chithra for £100.00 as he won a new expensive car in a competition. Did Michael intend to be legally bound by this promise to sell Chithra his BMW? Or was this simply a social agreement to a friend?

---
[139] (1925) AC 445

Intention to be legally bound generally differs depending on what kinds of agreements are being made. It is essential in forming a binding contract. Commercial agreements are decided upon a strong probability that the agreement was to be legally enforceable. In a social and domestic context there is a presumption that it is not intended to be legally binding. Therefore evidence to rebut the presumption should be provided. In **Lens v Devonshire Club**[140] where the winner of a golf competition held by a golf club could not file a claim for his prize in court due to the fact that, in the competition no one ever insinuated that there were legal implications. In advice to Michael, promising to sell his 3 year old BMW car to Chithra for £100.00, in the courts will not create an impulsion to be legally bound because it is a social agreement. *'to offer a friend a meal is not to invite litigation'*[141]. Therefore Michael's agreement may not be binding and he does not have to sell the BMW.

Enforceability of the promise to Rachel

On returning from his holiday, Michael promises Rachel, his daughter, £50.00 as she had cleaned his house for him whilst he was away. Can Rachel legally enforce this promise or has consideration past? If a person freely carries out an action of their own accord, after the other party makes a promise, then consideration is in the past. Therefore it is not valid. In the case of **Roscorla v Thomas**,[142] Roscorla brought a horse from Thomas'. After buying the horse it was promised that the horse was *"sound and free from vice"*. It materialised that the horse was vicious and the buyer sued. The court held that because the promise was made after the sale consideration was past and could not be enforced. Likewise, in **Re McArdle**[143] a daughter in law carried out improvements to a property. On completion the family agreed that she should be reimbursed the sum of £488, but the money was not paid. It was held that the promise to pay was unenforceable as it came after the work was completed. Past consideration is

---

[140] Unreported. See The Times Newspaper, December 4, 1914.
[141] G.C Cheshire, C.H. Fifoot and M.P.Furmston, Law of Contract, (15th Edn, OUP, 2007), 148.
[142] (1842) 3 QB 234
[143] [1951] Ch 669

generally seen to be something that purports invalid consideration. Using the above two authorities we can advise Michael that, the promise to pay constitutes past consideration. Therefore since the promise to pay Rachel has come after his return and after she has cleaned the house, then this establishes past consideration and he does not have to pay her.

The exception to this rule

There are certain exceptions to the past consideration rule. In **Lampleigh v Braithwait[144]**, the overwhelming majority of the judges assembled on the Common Bench held that *"where the promisor makes a request that the other do him some service, and (after the service is performed) promises to pay for it, the promise and the request go together and the contract is binding"*.[145] **Re Casey's Patents[146]** in a commercial context judgement held was despite the fact that the manager's consideration was past; the consideration had been produced in a business setting. This was also done at the owners own wishes and there was mutual understanding between both parties that the manager would get paid and also the further promise that he would be paid a predefined amount. In advice to Michael if Rachel has understood that she was to be paid for cleaning the house, she falls into the exception that consideration was past. It will largely depend on the judgement laid down by Lord Scarman above. Therefore Michael does not have to pay Rachel as Rachel's services has constituted past consideration.

Intention to create legal obligations

Another argument that Michael can raise in his defence is that there was never an intention to create legal obligations, because this is a social/domestic agreement in which a payment between a father and daughter should not be enforceable. In **Balfour v Balfour[147]** this was an agreement between a husband and wife,

---

[144] (1615) Hob 105
[145] Lampleigh v Braithwait(1615) Hob 105
[146] [1892] 1 Ch. 104
[147] [1919] 2 KB 571

who promised to pay £30 per month to his separated wife. It was held the wife could not recover the money because it was a domestic agreement and not legally binding. Furthermore in **Jones v Padavatton**[148] A mother offered her daughter an allowance if the daughter gave up her job in the US and studied for the Bar in London. The court held the agreement was vague and uncertain and therefore was a social arrangement. Using the above authorities it is likely on a balance of probabilities that the court will express this to be no more than a social agreement. Hence this agreement between Michael and Rachel is not enforceable.

Pay Daniel the addition £2000

Daniel is asking for more money for a job he is already contractually obliged to perform. Can he ask for the additional £2000 and is this an acceptable variation? Performing an action that is already required under a contract will not amount to valid consideration. The leading case on this issue is **Stilk v Myrick.**[149] In this case the court held that the crew had not provided consideration for additional payment of the deserted seamen's salary. The seamen were still under an obligation to carry out their pre-existing duties. In application to the facts of Michael's case it seems unlikely that Daniel would recover the additional £2,000. Michael could argue that Daniel merely discharged their pre-existing duty, and therefore no additional benefit was conferred on them. As a result, Michael may argue consideration was not present and the variation was therefore not binding.

Exceptions to the traditional consideration principle can be found in **Hartley v Ponsonby.**[150] A ship's crew was seriously unmanned and the captain promised the remaining crew members additional pay. The crew provided substantial consideration as it was dangerous to sail so understaffed and this was not within their contracts. It is unlikely that Daniel will be able to avail from this

---

[148] [1969] 1 W.L.R. 328
[149] 70 E.R. 1168;(1809)2 Camp 317
[150] (1857) 7 El &Bl 572

argument because the work has not been rendered completely different or extra and it cannot be said that a fresh contract has arisen in the circumstances.

In **Williams v Roffey Bros. & Nicholls (Contractors) Ltd**[151] the exception progressed further. A building contractor subcontracted with the claimant to carry out some carpentry work on a block of 27 flats being refurbished. For the carpentry work, Mr Williams was to be paid £20,000. Mr Williams ended up in financial difficulties even though he had already received £16,200. The building contractor pledged to pay Mr Williams extra for every flat he completes on time. This is because the company was worried they would be liable under a penalty clause for late completion and that the contract was priced too low. Mr Williams finished 8 flats, but had only received an additional £1,500 alone. The building contractors replaced Mr Williams with new carpenters and Mr Williams filed a claim. This is similarly related to **Stilk v Myrick**,[152] where again building contractors disputed that the claimant carried out tasks previously set out, that he was legally obliged to perform. On the other hand in **Williams v Roffey Bros.**[153] the courts adjudicated that the building contractor obtained practical benefits, not losing money under the penalty clause and avoided the disrupt effects of extra fees and the nuisance of finding a different contractor.[154] In **Williams v Roffey Bros**[155] Glidewell LJ delivered the primary evaluation on the theory established in **Stilk v Myrik**[156] Mr Williams had stipulated binding consideration even though he was performing a currently existing duty. Glidewell LJ developed on how the old principle had expanded, but his goal was not to change the old principle. He expressed that promissory estoppel had 'not yet been fully developed'. In addition he made the following points on existing law;

---

[151] [1990] 1 QB 1
[152] 70 E.R. 1168;(1809)2 Camp 317
[153] [1990] 1 QB 1
[154] Stone, Williams v Roffey: the death of Stilk v Myrick?, S.L. Rev. 1991, 2(Spr), 17-18
[155] [1990] 1 QB 1
[156] 70 E.R. 1168;(1809)2 Camp 317

1) *"If A enters into a contract with B to do work for, or to supply goods of services to B in return for payment by B and*
2) *At some point before A has finished performing his obligations that have been made out under the contract B has reason to doubt whether A will, or will be able to, complete his side of the bargain AND"*
3) *B then makes a promise to A to provide additional payment in return for A's promise to perform his contractual obligations on time AND"*
4) *As a result of giving his promise, B gets a benefit in practice, or obviates a disbenefit and*
5) *B's promise is not given as a result of economic duress of fraud on the part of A, THEN*
6) *The benefit to B is capable of being consideration for B's promise, so that the promise will be legally binding".* [157]

Therefore in relevance to this present case, it could be argued that Michael has received a practical benefit as the conservatory was built before his wife's birthday party. Nonetheless it is not clear that the principles in **Williams v Roffey**[158] would extend this far.[159] Whilst it is not addressed in the facts of our case, it may be that Michael wants no sign of building work if she is having guests over, which would not be there if the conservatory is built. This would certainly be a situation covered by the concept of practical benefit, although more details would be required to determine whether such practical benefits did arise.

Economic duress

For **Williams** to apply there must be an absence of economic

---

[157] [1990] 1 QB 1, pp. 15-16
[158] [1990] 1 QB 1
[159] South Caribbean Trading Ltd v TrafiguraBeheer [2004] EWHC 2676 (paras.106–09 of the judgment) in the Privy Council Colman J cast doubt on the decision in Williams v Roffey Bros.

duress. If's Daniel's behaviour can be categorised as illegitimate commercial pressure this would either render the contract void or simply be *'the rough and tumble of normal commercial bargaining'*[160]. Absence of economic duress would allow Daniel to recover the £2000. Michael reluctantly agreed to pay the additional money not wanting to upset the birthday plans. In **DSND Subsea Ltd v Petroleum Geo-Services ASA**[161] in which Dyson J stated that;

> *"[...] there must be pressure,*
> *(a) whose practical effect is that there is compulsion on, or lack of practical choice for, the victim,*
> *(b) which is illegitimate, and*
> *(c) which is a significant cause inducing the claimant to enter into the contract."*[162]

It is therefore debatable whether the lack of practical choice or compulsion was illegitimate, it would be inaccurate to determine whether the application of pressure is to be expected in this kind of environment. In reference to this case, Daniel must prove that Michael has a realistic alternative but chose to appease the pressure he was involved in. Daniel must show he was acting in good faith and Michael did not protest the variation. Otherwise this would lead to breach of contract by Daniel.

Promissory estoppel

The doctrine of promissory estoppel applies where; *"a promise was made which was intended to create legal relations and which, to the knowledge of the person making the promise, was going to be acted on by the person to whom it was made and which was in fact so acted on"*.[163] The dispute is that Michael can be seen to have made an unequivocal promise, which was intended to legally affect both parties. Daniel stated that he would finish before Michael's wife's birthday party for the extra £2000. In Michael's

---

[160] DSND Subsea Ltd v Petroleum Geo-Services ASA [2000] All ER (D) 1101
[161] [2000] All ER (D) 1101
[162] ibid.
[163] Central London Property Trust v High Trees House Ltd [1947] KB 130.

acceptance Daniel would have relied on this promise. Initial requirements are that it should be inequitable for the promisor to invalidate the promise **D & C Builders v Rees**[164]. It is arguable that it is unfair for Michael to go back on their agreement to pay the additional £2,000 to Daniel. However, promissory estoppel cannot be used as a separate cause of action[165]. This would prove challenging for Daniel to recover the £2000. First Daniel could claim relying on Michael's promise and use estoppel as a defence that he was still bound to the terms of the initial agreement. Second is that Daniel can prove he supplied valid consideration for the promise to pay the additional £2,000 by using **Wiliams**.

Conclusion

Overall this advice for Michael consists of the following. Consideration must be sufficient and of some benefit or detriment to each party[166]. Michael has given sufficient consideration and would be legally enforced to sell his 3 year old BMW to Chithra as it has been established that it is worth £100 which is of some value. In social and domestic agreements the courts assumption is that they are not intended to be legally binding. This means that in concern of the same issue through the principle of intention to create legal obligations. Michael does not have to sell his 3 year old BMW to Chithra for £100 because this was a social agreement which the courts would assume neither Michael nor Chithra intended it to be legally enforceable. The promise for Rachel cleaning his house for £50.00 is enforceable relies on the principle of whether Rachel's act can be determined as past consideration. In this instance because Rachel's act was done on return of her father this constitutes past consideration.[167] Moreover, the court will express this as a social agreement hence not enforceable. In respect of Daniel, he may be able to recover the £2,000 from Michael on the basis that fresh consideration was present. Whilst being weak this argument is a question of fact. Daniel may choose to rely on the case of **Wllliams v Roffey** in establishing that

---

[164] [1966] 2 QB 617.
[165] Combe v Combe [1951] 2 KB 215.
[166] Currie v Misa [1875] LR 10 Ex 153, 162.
[167] Roscorla v Thomas (1842) 3 QB 234.

Michael received a practical benefit from the conservatory being finished in time for his wife's birthday. In order for Daniel to rely on the practice benefit doctrine he will have to show the absence of economic duress. It seems clear that economic duress was not present. The doctrine of promissory estoppel will not be of any use to Daniel because it can only be used as a shield and not a sword. This advice has given a firm conclusion in respect of each point on the information we have before us.

Chapter 8   Privity of Contract

Introduction

It is a fundamental principle of English law that no one can derive rights or obligations from a contract to which he has given no consideration and is hence not a party. This doctrine, known as privity of contract, is still substantially valid but has been modified in various ways. In a number of situations, some parties are third parties to contracts. Nevertheless, they can still gain rights and certain liabilities as more distant parties and, in some cases, even if they are not party to the original contract at all.

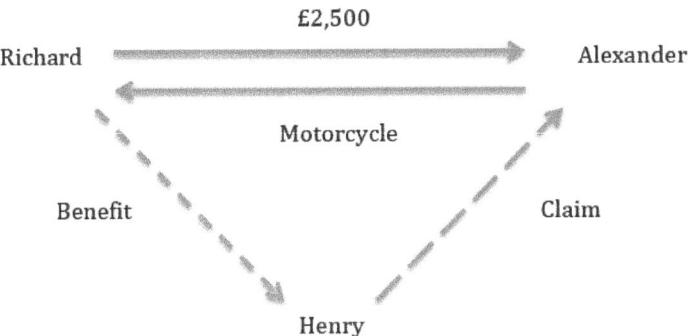

There have been multiple criticisms of the doctrine of privity and its associated common law exceptions. Some argue the privity rule enables parties to circumvent contractual obligations intended to benefit an outside party, while disregarding the decisions of the original parties. It can also prevent the victimised party from suing the party who is truly responsible, which can create multiple lawsuits focused on settling one issue. Additionally, the sheer number of exceptions to the doctrine of privity has been condemned as overly complex and contradictory; however, the Rights of Third Parties Act 1999 succeeded in clarifying the rights of a third party in a contract.

Question and Answer

- Privity of Contract Problem question

Privity of Contract Problem question

Question

Jo books a holiday to Italy for her and her family through a tour operator based in the UK. She specifies that the accommodation must provide facilities for young children. When Jo and her family arrive they are told that their specified accommodation is no longer available. The tour company offer Jo alternative accommodation located in the city centre. Due to its location the alternative accommodation does not provide any facilities for children; in fact, guests must be at least 18 years old in order to stay at this alternative accommodation.

Jo brings an action for breach of contract against the tour company claiming damages for the ruined holiday for herself and on behalf of her family.

Discuss the legal issues.

Answer

Introduction

This is an advice that discusses the legal issues in relation to Jo who books a holiday to Italy for her and her family through a tour operator based in the UK. This paper will highlight and critically discuss all the legal issue that arise. It will start by discussing the liability of the tour operator, for the additional cost of accommodation incurred by Jo. It will then look at liability of the tour operator for disappointment or 'mental distress' or loss of amenity caused by the ruined holiday. It will examine the case of **Jarvis v Swans Tours Ltd**[168], which is a similar fact authority. It will then examine the issue of privity of contract and how this stops Jo from bringing an action on behalf of her family. It will then discuss the case of **Jackson v Horizon Holidays Ltd**[169], to show

---

[168] [1972] EWCA Civ 8, first instance
[169] [1975] 1 WLR 1468

how the rule of privity was circumvented. This paper will then examine the Contract (Rights of Third Parties) Act 1999, to see how Jo can rely on this to claim damages for her family. Lastly this paper will conclude its findings.

Liability of the tour operator

Ultimately Jo is unhappy with what she has received under the contract for her holiday. The legal issue is whether she can claim damages for her loss. She cannot repudiate the contact for the holiday because she has received some of the benefit.[170] She booked a family holiday. The hotel she booked was no longer available. It can be argued this is a breach of warranty.[171] A breach of warranty entitles the innocent part to damages.[172] The tour company makes an attempt to remedy the situation by offering an alternative hotel. The hotel however, did not offer facilities for children. Moreover, the hotel did not accept guests under the age of 18. This is a breach of contract. The breach fundamentally alters the nature of the contract. This means Jo has to find alternative accommodation. Jo can sue the tour operator for i) cost of hotel; ii) any additional expense; and iii) loss of enjoyment or distress. She will have to satisfy the principles of remoteness, causation and mitigation.

(i)   Recovering the cost of alternative accommodation

The purpose of contractual damages is to put the party back in the position had the breach of contract not occurred. Jo can recover the cost of finding new accommodation. Hotel can be quite expensive at short notice. If this cost of Jo's hotel outweighs the cost of the initial holiday, the court may award here a difference in value between the performance received and that promised in the contract (diminution in value), i.e. a difference in value between what way paid for the holiday and what it was worth. In **Jarvis v Swans Tours Ltd**[173] the judge in the court of first instance

---

[170] This is known as a quantum meruit. See Sumpter v. Hedges (1898) 1 QB 673
[171] Section 62 of the Sale of Goods Act 1979 states a warranty is 'collateral to the main purpose of the contract'.
[172] Bettini v Gye (1876) 1 QBD 183
[173] [1972] EWCA Civ 8

believed Mr. Jarvis had got half of what he paid for. So the judge gave him half the amount which he had paid.

Another example is the case of **Ruxley Electronics and Construction Ltd v Forsyth**.[174] The court decided in Ruxley that it would be unreasonable to claim the cost of cure as the relation between the work fulfilled and the benefit obtained would be unfair to the defendant and therefore a difference in value should be awarded. [175] In that sense Jo is likely to be awarded the difference in value in what her holiday was worth and what she received.

(ii) Additional expense

Moreover, if Jo has incurred additional expenses, i.e. taxi fares to and from the new hotel which are also recoverable.

(iii) Damages for disappointment or 'mental distress' or loss of amenity

The question arises if Jo can claim for mental distress, anguish or annoyance caused by breach of contract? The authority of **Addis v Gramophone Co Ltd**[176] says that usually for mental distress, anguish or annoyance caused by breach of contract damages are not awarded. The House of Lords has refused to award damages in Addis v Gramophone Co Ltd that has been created as to the 'harsh and humiliating' way the defendant has released the Addis from his job in breach of contract. The House of Lords again confirmed their decision in **Johnson v Unisys Ltd**[177] by stating that "damages for distress and injury to feelings resulting from the manner of dismissal are unavailable in the law of contract"[178].

Nevertheless, as to most rules, there are also exceptions to this rule. In a small number of cases, which have had the main purpose of relaxation, pleasure and peace of mind mental distress may be

---

[174] [1996] A.C. 344
[175] McMeel, Gerard, Common sense on cost of cure, L.M.C.L.Q. 1995, 4(Nov), 456-461
176 [1909] AC 488
177 [2001] UKLH 13
178 Lord Hoffmann in Johnson v Unisys Limited [2001] UKHL 13

compensated,[179] as stated also confirmed more recently in **Farley v Skinner**[180]. The House of Lords in **Farley** stated damaged could be recovered where a major object (though not the whole purpose) of the contract was to provide pleasure, relaxation and peace of mind".[181]

This can also be seen from the authority of **Jarvis v Swans Tours Ltd**[182] in which a brochure has promised a holiday with an enjoyable time but in fact it fell short of the promise. Jarvis has then sued for his disappointment and the Court of Appeal decided that damages for Jarvis' disappointment and distress can be awarded in circumstances like this. Lord Denning MR remarked that the decision in Addis that under the above stated circumstances damages may not be awarded is out of date. Furthermore he said that in terms of holiday contracts or other contracts which promise enjoyment and entertainment exceptions should be made.

Another authority which can be brought into relation with Jo's case is **Jackson v Horizon Holidays Ltd**[183]. Mr Jackson has purchased a holiday from Horizon Holidays Ltd which has promised in their brochure the accommodation to have excellent facilities, but when Jackson has arrived with his family the hotel's facilities were substandard. Lord Denning MR stated in his judgement: *"they were greatly disappointed. Their room had not got a connecting door with the room for the children at all. The room for the children was mildewed - black with mildew, at the bottom. There was fungus growing on the walls. The toilet was stained. The shower was dirty. There was no bath. They could not let the children sleep in it...They were so uncomfortable at Brown's Hotel, that after a fortnight they moved to the Pegasus Reef Hotel."*[184] The judge had followed the authority of **Jarvis v Swans Tours Ltd** and the judge awarded just a little bit less than the initial cost of the holiday as damages in distress. In Jarvis Lord Denning

---

179 Jarvis v Swan Tours [1973] 1 All ER 71
180 [2001] UKHL 49
181 Pearce, David, Farley v Skinner: right or wrong?, C.L.J. 2002, 61(1), 24-27
182 [1972] EWCA Civ 8
183 [1975] 1 WLR
184 [1975] 1 WLR

MR held that Mr Jarvis could recover damages for the cost of his holiday, but also damages for "disappointment, the distress, the upset and frustration caused by the breach

In light of the authorities Jo will be able be able to recover damages for mental distress, anguish or annoyance caused by breach of contract, because the whole purpose of the contract was to provide pleasure and relaxation in the form of a holiday for Jo and her children. The fact that when Jo and her family arrive at the hotel they are told that their specified accommodation is no longer available appears to be a breach of warranty that can be remedied if alternative accommodation is provided.

Privity of contract

One problem Jo faces is claiming damages on behalf of her family. It can be argued that the family was not in contract with the tour operator and thus cannot enforce the contract against them. The doctrine of privity of contract, a fundamental principle in common law, says though, that a rights and obligations created by contracts are only applicable to the parties of the contract.[185] This means that it does not confer enforceable rights or impose any obligations on a person who is not a party to the contract.[186] How then can Jo's family bring an action? One possibility is Jo can bring it on their behalf as in the case of **Jackson v Horizon Holidays Ltd**.[187]

Circumventing Privity: Jackson v Horizon Holidays Ltd

As already addressed above, the authority of Jackson is highly relevant to Jo's case. The Jackson case is representing the difficulties with the general principle of privity in a family context. The court's decision in Jackson was that when the buyer of a holiday contracts for the benefit of himself and his family, then the buyer may be able to sue for his family. Jo, can according to the authority of Jackson, sue for damages suffered by her family as

---

[185] Flannigan, Robert (October 1987). "Privity - the end of an era (error)". Law Quarterly Review p.103
[186] Dean, Meryll (2000) Removing a blot on the landscape - the reform of the doctrine of privity. Journal of Business Law, March. pp. 143-152
[187] [1975] 1 WLR

well as for herself. This exception to the principle of privity is therefore applicable in the sense that the family was not a party to the contract and not able to sue for damages by themselves for want of not being one of the contracting parties. [188]

The Contract (Rights of Third Parties) Act 1999

The Jackson case has been decided 1975, which has been before the implementation of the Rights of Third Parties Act in 1999. If it would have been decided after 1999, it would now be partly resolved by the Act's section 1(1) (b). The Act permits Jo's family to sue for the damages by themselves. This is an enormous change to the rule of privity which has been undertaken as to the concerns of the judiciary and the Law Commission to review the rule of privity.[189] Though the Act only allows special circumstances, a third party to enforce terms of contracts to which they are not a party.[190] In that sense, Jo's family may now after the implementation of the Act enforces a term of the contract to which only Jo is a contracting party but the contract cannot be enforced against Jo's family. In s.1 of the Act, a two-limbed test is used in order to find out whether the third party can sue for a contract or not.[191]

Jo's family may enforce the term if: i) The contract expressly says that they may (section 1(1)(a)); or ii) it purports to confer a benefit upon them (section 1(1)(b)) unless, if on a proper construction of the contract (s1(2)) it is clear that the parties, Jo and the tour operator, did not intend the term to be enforceable by the third party, meaning the family. For section 1(1)(b) to apply, it must be established that the agreement indeed 'intended to confer a benefit' on Jo's family.[192] Furthermore, it can be found in section 1(3) that

---

[188] Jacobs, Edward (1986). "Judicial reform of privity and consideration". Journal of Business Law (6):
[189] Bridge, Michael (2001). "Privity of contract; Third parties", Edinburgh Law Review 5 (1): 85–102
[190] Flannigan, Robert (October 1987). "Privity – the end of an era (error)". Law Quarterly Review 103 (4): 564–593
[191] MacMillan, Catharine (2000). "A Birthday Present for Lord Denning: The Contracts (Rights of Third Parties) Act 1999". Modern Law Review 63 (5): 721–738
[192] Dolphin & Maritime & Aviation Services Ltd v Sveriges Angfartygs Assurans Forening, The

Jo's family would have to be expressly identified. This would have to be done either by description, by being a member of a class or simply by name. This was applied in the authority of **Avraamides and another v Colwill and Another**.[193] There has been a transfer agreement and Lord Justice Waller held that it did not confer a benefit to the Avraamides as they have not been expressly identified in accordance with section 1(3).[194]

Conclusion

Moreover, the question arises if Jo could recover the full expenses. According to the authority of **Ruxley** she would not be obliged to the full price of the booked holiday paid and the full price of the alternative accommodation and the extra expenses but she may be able to recover the difference between the original price paid and the final expenses, in that sense the difference in value. She will also be able to recover the additional expenses and damages for mental distress, anguish or annoyance as the purpose of the contract was to provide pleasure and relaxation. Additionally it is essential to identify her family relevant third parties and whether they should be given enforceable rights in order to draw the right conclusions with the use of the Act. Moreover, it should be questioned whether, when third parties receive enforceable rights, there ability on enforcing these rights should be restricted.

Swedish Club [2009] EWHC 716 (Comm) summarised in Poole's Textbook on Contract Law (Chapter 11)
[193] [2006] EWCA civ 1533
[194] Furmston, Michael (2007). Law of Contract (15th ed.), Oxford University Press

Chapter 9   Terms of Contract

The duties and obligations of each party to the contract are laid out in the terms of a contract. These terms of contract can be **express terms** laid down by the parties themselves, or **implied terms** which are inferred from the intention of the parties and facts of the agreement.

Question and Answers

- Problem question on implied terms

Problem question on implied terms

Question

On 1 August 2019, Adam purchases and takes possession of a studio flat in Islington. He subsequently visits DanishDesign Ltd, a furniture shop in South Kensington, where he finds on display a sofa he likes. The sofa, a model "Copenhagen", is designed by the famous Isben Isbesen. Adam tests the sofa, and based on the way it looks and feels, decides to place an order for "Copenhagen 3-seater black sofa with sofa bed". While the display model is in fact a "Copenhagen 2-seater white sofa (no sofa bed)", the sales assistant explains that the model Adam orders is "more or less the same" as the one on display.

Adam pays £5000 in cash for the sofa and an extra £250 for delivery (£5250 in total). DanishDesign Ltd promises Adam that his new sofa will be delivered to his Islington flat and assembled on site by Saturday, 28th September 2019.

DanishDesign Ltd emails Adam on Friday, 27th September 2019 to say that the sofa will be delivered on Monday, 30th September 2019. DanishDesign explains that deliveries are only made on weekdays in London (Monday – Friday).

The sofa is delivered and unpacked. Once it's assembled, Adam realises the sofa is a "Copenhagen 2-seater white sofa (no sofa bed)". Furious, Adam returns to the DanishDesign furniture shop. He agrees with the Shop Manager that he will keep the delivered sofa until a replacement with sofa bed can be delivered.

On 10th October 2019, DanishDesign Ltd delivers a replacement: a "Copenhagen 3-seater black sofa with sofa bed". After using the sofa bed for a week the sofa begins to creak; now he wishes to return the sofa and get his money back. DanishDesign Ltd refuses.

Advise the parties assuming Adam is a non-consumer buyer.

Explain how, if at all, your advice would differ if Adam were

89

'consumer' in this transaction.

Answer

This is an advice for all the parties. The advice will deal with both satiations of Adam being a non-consumer (business) and a consumer. If Adam is dealing with DanishDesign Ltd ("DD") as a non-consumer then the Sale of Goods Act 1979 ("SGA 1979") applies to 'contracts of sale of goods'.[195] If Adam is a consumer his rights will be protected under the Consumer Rights Act 2015 ("CRA 2015").

DD promises Adam that his new sofa will be delivered on 28th September 2019. They then email Adam to say that the sofa will be delivered on Monday, 30th September 2019. In international sales contracts the date of shipment shapes part of the goods description. In **Bowes** v. **Shand**[196] it was held that early shipment of goods was as bad as late ones. Whether shipment is early or late under s.13 SGA 1979 it is in breach of implied term and in breach of contract. However in a domestic non-consumer contract time is unlikely to be of the essence. This means that DD changing the delivery date will be deemed a breach of warranty rather than a breach of condition, because it does not go to the heart of the contract and deprive Adam of the benefit he will confer under the contract.[197] Thus if Adam has to take the day off work on Monday to be at home for delivery then his loss of wages will be recoverable in damages. Adam cannot reject the contact. If Adam is a consumer the CRA 2015[198] there is a short term right to reject. There is a default delivery period of thirty days, during which DD have to deliver the goods unless a lengthier period has been agreed.[199] We have not been told if delivery is time essential and if another practical delivery time cannot be agreed, then Adam has the right cancel the order for a complete refund.

---

[195] s.1 SGA 1979
[196] (1877) 2 App Cas 455
[197] Hong Kong Fir Shipping v Kawasaki Kisen Kaisha [1962] 2 QB 26
[198] s.20(1) Consumer Rights Act 2015
[199] s.22(3) Consumer Rights Act 2015

The sofa is delivered and is not a Copenhagen 3-seater with sofa bed. There is an implied term under s.13 SGA 1979 that goods sold under contract will correlate to the description. This is actionable under the s.13 provisions.[200] However, Adam has asked for the wrong goods to be changed and replaced with a "Copenhagen 3-seater black sofa with sofa bed". The breach of an express term, gives rises to repudiation with damages, nonetheless if the term is a warranty this gives rise to just damages. This is a breach of condition but Adam had treated this breach of implied term as a breach of warranty and asked for it to be remedied. If Adam is dealing as a consumer under s.11(1) CRA 2015 *'every contract to supply goods by description is to be treated as including a term that the goods will match the description'*. Under s.19(3) CRA 2015 it states that if the goods do not conform to their description Adam has the right to repair or replacement.[201]

After a week the sofa starts to creak. Adam had tested the sofa, and was told the model he orders will be "more or less the same" as the one on display. Adam now wishes to return the sofa and get his money back. The general principle is there is a term implied by law into non-consumer contracts that offers minim protection to the consumer that when goods are brought by sample they will correspond with that sample. Under s.15(2) SGA 1979 if something is not 'as per sample', the contracted quantity can be rejected due to not matching the sample. The leading case on this is **Ruben v. Faire Bros & Co Ltd**[202] in which the buyer was sold rubber material from the seller. The rubber however, did not match the sample, which was flat and soft. It was argued by the seller that through a simple process it could be put right, but the court held under s.15 it was a breach due to the delivered goods not matching the sample. Using the above law we can advise Adam that the Copenhagen 3-seater black sofa must correspond to the sample he saw in the shop. Section 15(A) SGA 1979 states if there is a breach of implied term but if the breach is so slight that it is unreasonable to reject then the buyer will only be entitled

---

[200] Ashington Piggeries Ltd v. Christopher Hill Ltd [1972] AC 441
[201] s.23 Consumer Rights Act 2015
[202] [1949] 1 All ER 215

to compensation.[203] The burden of proof is on the seller to show s.15(A) should apply.[204][205] Adam may be able to argue against the sellers assertions that the breach is not so slight. If Adam is dealing as a consumer s.14(1) CRA 2015 states goods by reference to a model seen or examined by the consumer before entering into the contract the good must correspond to the model.

The sofa starting to creak also goes to its quality. Moreover, in a contract of sale where the seller is selling in the course of a business there is also an implied term that the goods will be of quality which is satisfactory.[206] Satisfactory quality is what a "reasonable person" would objectively regard as satisfactory, taking into account "the price, description, and other circumstances."[207] This is stated at s.14 (2B) SGA which provides five aspects, which is a non-exhaustive list: one of them being "b) fitness of all the purposes for which goods are commonly supplied". In **Australian Knitting Mills Ltd. v. Grant**[208] the case concerned underwear that caused dermatitis. The court clarified the definition. It was held by Dixon J that the *"definition should be read as allowing the buyer to acquaint facts of the goods and any hidden defects that exist"*. Thus having a sofa that creaks when you sit on it is not fit for the purpose for which it is being supplied and hence "unsatisfactory". This breach of this implied term gives rise for Adam to repudiate the contract and get his money back.

DD refuses to return the goods. The argument that they will advance is the contract was formed on or around 1 August 2019 and rejection is now coming around 17th October 2019 more than two months after the purchase and have thus accepted the contract. If the court finds that the buyer has accepted the goods then the buyer loses the right to reject for a beach of condition. Under s.35 SGA 1979 it states *"the buyer has accepted the goods if they have intimated their acceptance, or if the buyer does an act that is*

---

[203] 15(A)(1)(b) SGA 1979
[204] 15(A)(3) SGA 1979
[205] Moore & Co. v. Landauer & Co. [1921] 2 KB 519
[206] This replaced "merchantable quality"
[207] s.14(2A) SGA 1979
[208] Australian Knitting Mills Ltd. v. Grant [1933] 50 C.L.R. 387

inconsistent with the ownership of the seller, or a reasonable time has lapsed". What is reasonable time? The case of Bernstein v. Pamson Motors (Golders Green) Ltd[209] relates to reasonable time. The produced argument was that the buyer had the goods delivered to him and he had a period of time to examine them. It was found by the High Court that 28 days was more than reasonable time. DD will argue that because Adam has accepted the previous breach where he was delivered the wrong sofa this constitutes acceptance in relation to the new sofa. This argument is likely to fail because it goes against common sense in that the buyer will not be entitled to examine the goods to see their suitability. Moreover, DD should not be entitled to relying on Adam waiver of their previous breaches to be evidence of affirmation of the contract.

Under the CRA 2015 the implied terms Adam can expect in relation to goods are taken from those contained in the SGA 1979 these include implied terms that the goods will be fit for purpose,[210] match their description[211] and are of satisfactory quality.[212] The right to reject follows after any breach of the implied terms.[213] There is a short–term right to reject under the CRA 2015.[214] Exercising the short–term right to rejects time limit is *"the end of the thirty days beginning with the first day after all these has happened: a) ownership or possession in the goods has been transferred to the consumer; b) he goods have been delivered; and c) where the contract requires the seller to install the goods or take other action"*.[215] There is a time limit of thirty days in which a buyer is able to reject goods prior to something mentioned in (a)-(c) happening.[216] Adam still has a right to reject. Any refund that may be owed to him may be lowered by a deduction for use, to reflect the use he has had since the goods were delivered.[217] However, the deduction needs to take into

---

[209] [1987] 2 All ER 220
[210] s.10(3) Consumer Rights Act 2015
[211] s.11(1) Consumer Rights Act 2015
[212] s.9(1) and (2) Consumer Rights Act 2015
[213] s.19(6) Consumer Rights Act 2015
[214] s.20(1) Consumer Rights Act 2015
[215] s.22(3)(a)(b)(c) Consumer Rights Act 2015
[216] s.22(3) Consumer Rights Act 2015
[217] s.24(8) Consumer Rights Act 2015

account the use in the period where the buyer only has the goods due to DD's failing to collect the goods at the specified time.[218] If the final right to reject has been exercised in the first six months then no deduction can be made. For this reason, the first six months means six months starting with the first day after all of the prior mentioned in (a)-(c) (above) has occurred. Adam will be able to reject the sofa as he intends and get his money back.

Chapter 9 - Classification of Contractual terms of the Contract

- **Condition**
- **Warranty**
- **Innonomiate terms**

The law classifies the terms of the contract according to their importance and for this there are three kinds of contractual terms: conditions, warranties and innominate terms.

Question and Answers

- Terms of Contract Essay Question
- Terms of Contract Problem Question

---

[218] s.24(9) Consumer Rights Act 2015

Terms of Contract Essay Question

Question

Evaluate the importance of terms within a contract according to their importance to the contract and the method of origin and consequence of breach.

Answer

Introduction

This essay will discuss the traditional view which is that each term of a contract, express or implied, is either a **condition** or a **warranty**, depending upon its importance with regard to the purpose of the contract. The question whether a term is a **condition** or a warranty becomes significant in cases of breach of contract.

The distinction between a condition and a warranty is that a condition is an important term 'going to the root of the contract'. On the other hand, a **warranty** is described under s. 61 of the Sale of Goods Act 1979 as:

> "an agreement with reference to goods which are the subject of a contract of sale, but collateral to the main purpose of such contract, the breach of which gives rise to a claim for damages, but not a right to reject the goods and treat the contract as repudiated".

As a general principle, if a promisor breaks a condition in any respect, however slight, the other party has a right to elect to treat himself as discharged from future obligations under the contract and to sue for damages immediately. If he does not exercise the right to elect to treat the contract as at an end (instead choosing to affirm the contract) he will remain bound by the contract, but can sue for damages with respect to the other party's breach. If, on the other hand, a promisor breaks a warranty in any respect, the only remedy available to the other party is to sue for damages; i.e. there is no right to treat the contract as at an end.

Deciding whether it is a condition or warranty

Since there is a stronger remedy available for breach of condition than for breach of warranty, it is not unusual for the parties to be in dispute as to whether a term is a condition or a warranty. The difference is conveniently illustrated by the following cases.

In **Poussard v Spiers and Pond** (1876) 1 QBD 410: an actress was under a contractual obligation to play the leading role in an opera as from the beginning of its London run. Owing to illness the actress could not attend the last rehearsal or the first four performances, and when she offered to take her part in the fifth performance the producers refused. The actress sued for wrongful dismissal, but the court said her participation in the first four performances was a **condition** fundamental to the contract, and its breach entitled the producers to treat the contract as terminated.

In **Bettini v Gye** (1876) 1 QBD 183: a singer was under contractual obligation to sing in a series of concerts and to take part in six days of rehearsals before the first performance. He arrived three days late, thus leaving only three days for rehearsals. The judge said this was not a fundamental condition. The undertaking to take part in the rehearsals for six days was a warranty and not a condition. The breach entitled the other party to damages but not to repudiate the contract.

Calling it a "Term or Condition"

The parties to the contract are free to classify the relative importance of the terms of their contract. However, even where the parties describe a term as a condition it is open to the court to hold that the parties could not have intended the term to have this effect.

One example of this is seen in **Schuler v Wickman Machine**

Tool Sales [1974] AC 235: Wickman was given sole distribution rights in the UK of Schuler's panel presses for a period of four and a half years. Clause 7(b) of the agreement provided that:

> *'It shall be **condition** of this agreement that (i) (Wickman) shall send its representatives to visit (the six large UK motor manufacturers) at least once in every week for the purpose of soliciting orders for panel presses...'*

Wickman's representatives failed to make a number of these visits and Schuler claimed that this failure was a breach of condition under clause 7(b) and, as such, was a material breach, as defined under clause 11(a) of the agreement, which entitled Schuler to determine the agreement. It was held by the House of Lords that clause 7(b) was not a condition as the parties could not have intended that a single breach, however trivial, would entitle the innocent party to terminate the contract.

The House of Lords in this case ignored the clear wording of the contract, ostensibly on the grounds that to interpret the particular clause as a condition was so unreasonable that it could not have been intended by the parties. However, Lord Wilberforce, in a dissenting judgment, was of the opinion that the express use of the word 'condition' should have been conclusive of the matter. Undoubtedly, if the use of the word 'condition' is not conclusive of the matter then this will create problems of uncertainty, not least that the innocent party will be unsure as to whether he has the right to terminate the contract for breach of that term.

The modern approach

The traditional distinction between conditions and warranties is no longer regarded as exhaustive. In **Hong Kong Fir Shipping Co v Kawasaki Kisen Kaishi Ltd.** [1961] 2 Lloyd's Rep 478 the Court of Appeal held that there are many terms which at the outset are neither conditions nor warranties but are of **an innominate or intermediate nature**. A minor breach of such a term will only amount to a breach of warranty but a serious breach thereof will allow the innocent party to terminate the contract and claim damages. This represents a more flexible approach and allows the court a good deal of leeway when dealing with cases where the purported innocent party is attempting to use a trivial breach in order to extract themselves from a contractual agreement which is no longer commercially advantageous.

In the **Hong Kong Fir** case the Court of Appeal took the view that the legal consequences of a breach of contract depend on the consequences of the breach or, to use the words of Diplock LJ 'the nature of the event to which the breach gives rise.' This is quite different from the traditional approach based on the distinction between minor terms (warranties) and important terms (conditions); the distinction resting on the intention of the parties at the time they made their contract. Admittedly, this analysis may promote justice as between the parties but such justice is achieved at the cost of certainty, in particular certainty as to whether the innocent party has the right to terminate the contract as a result of the breach.

Terms of Contract Problem Question

Question

Fred advertises in an antiques journal that he has an aeroplane for sale. The advertisement appears on 1 October and reads:

"A rare opportunity to acquire a collector's item: A bi-plane which belonged to the early flying ace, Sir George Ditcher, has come on the market for the first time. Sir George was an early member of the Royal Flying Corps and was the person upon whom Wiggles, the fictional flying hero, was based. £85,000 or nearest offer."

Boris, the owner of a museum dedicated to items connected with the First World War, contacts Fred on 15 October to discuss the sale. Fred shows Boris a large collection of letters written by Sir George Ditcher which describe an aeroplane of the same type as the one offered for sale as 'my little buzz bomb'. He also points out numerous letters written to Sir George by the author of the Wiggles books. On 31 October, Boris agrees to buy the aeroplane for £85,000 and a brief written contract is entered into which makes no mention of Sir George Ditcher or Wiggles.

Boris displays the bi-plane at his museum describing it as 'previously owned by Sir George Ditcher, the real life Wiggles'. It has now been established that, although he did fly it, the aeroplane never belonged to Sir George Ditcher and that there ten other people who had as strong a claim as Sir George Ditcher to be the basis of the Wiggles character.

Advise Boris.

Answer

Introduction

This paper aims to advise Boris of his position within the sale of a bi-plane, allegedly owned by Sir George Ditcher, for the sum of £85,000. After the sale, Boris discovered that the statements relating to Sir George Ditcher are unlikely to have been true. We will identify the potential issues and assess whether Boris is likely to have claim on the basis that the statements concerning Sir George Ditcher are terms of the contract.

1. Importance of the statement of sale regarding Sir George Ditcher.
2. Skill & knowledge of the defendant.
3. The written contract.
4. Conditions and warranties of their contract.
5. A modern approach to conditions and warranties.
6. Identify potential claim / conclusion

For Boris to have claim against Fred upon the discovery of the statement identifying Sir George Ditcher as the previous owner of the plane for sale and the relevance of the Wiggles books being based upon it would need to be identified that the above is, for all legal intents and purposes, not only a term of their contract of sale but whether this term is deemed to be a condition under the contract or a warranty.

1. Importance of the statement of sale regarding Sir George Ditcher.

Fred advertised the bi-plane for sale and in the advertisement states that "[the bi-plane] belonged to the flying ace, Sir George Ditcher, has come on the market for the first time". For this to be interpreted as a valid term of the contract, Boris would have to have made it clear that without this statement he would not have been interested in the purchase of Fred's bi-plane. The authority for this is in Bannerman v White where it was held that the plaintiff could claim for breach of contract on the basis that if the statement regarding the products quality were not made, they would not have bothered to inquire about the price. From the information provided we cannot determine whether Boris made any statement regarding the importance of the planes history (in regards to Sir George Ditcher).

Contrary to the above, Fred's lawyers may suggest that due to the subject matter (that of a plane nearing 100 years old), it would be implied that further verification would be required. The authority for this is in **Ecay v Godfrey** where the court held that in certain situations, it would be 'normally expected' that further investigation would be required. From this we can suggest that if there were no other mitigating terms, it would have been Boris's responsibility to independently verify the statements made by Fred.

2. Skill & knowledge of the defendant.

Fred produced a large collection of letters written by Sir George Ditcher which was claimed to be evidence describing the plane he was selling and a number of letters from the author of the Wiggles books to Sir George Ditcher (who at the time was claimed to be the inspiration for the books). Due to Boris's professional standing, that is the owner of a museum dedicated to items connected with the First World War, these can be identified as mere representations. The authority for this is in **Oscar Chess Ltd v Williams** where it was held that the seller of a vintage car, being sold to a dealer, was not responsible for an inaccuracy of the age as it was true to the best of his knowledge and based on information perceived to be true. While we do not know of Fred's qualification, we can assume that Boris is considered to be an expert in the field in which he owns a museum to collect similar items.

3. The written contract.

Boris and Fred enter into a 'brief' written contract to conduct the sale of the plane however this makes no mention of Sir George Ditcher or Wiggles. For the aforesaid statements to be considered terms of the contract it would require that they be shown to have been of the utmost importance. We can see this in **Evans & Sons Ltd v Andrea Merzarlo Ltd** where the court of appeal decided that because the plaintiff had specified the importance of the cargo not being carried 'on deck' and that the defendant had given oral assurance of this, that it was to be considered a term of the contract and overrule the standard contract. From the above we can see that if the importance of the statements relating to Sir George Ditcher where either made apparent or can be objectively seen as being apparent, they may be deemed a term of the contract. From the outset we can see the relevance in that the statement was used as a way of attracting potential buyers.

4. Conditions and warranties of their contract

For this term to be considered a condition of the contract it would need to be a term 'going to the root of the contract'. We can see this in **Poussard v Spiers and Pond** where it was held that due to the plaintiff being unable to attend the last rehearsal and first four performances, she had effectively breached a condition of her contract and the producers where able to terminate the contract.

Contrary to the above, a warranty is described by S.61 of the Sale of Goods Act 1979 as:

"an agreement with reference to goods which are the subject of a contract of sale, but collateral to the main purpose of such contract, the breach of which gives rise to a claim for damages, but not a right to reject the goods and treat the contract as repudiated".

This can been seen in **Bettini v Gye** where it was held that a singer who had missed 3 days of a contracted 6 days of rehearsal was a trivial breach that would attract a claim for damages and not repudiate the contract.

5. The modern approach to conditions and warranties

The above is considered to be the traditional approach to what a condition and warranty are, due to the nature of the subject matter it is a possibility that it would be unconscionable for the contract to be repudiated on the basis of a breach of terms. This can be seen in **Hong Kong Fir Shipping Co v Kawasaki Kisen Kaishi Ltd** where the Court of appeal held that some terms are of "an innominate or intermediate nature" and that a minor breach of terms would amount to a breach of warranty but a serious breach would allow the innocent party to terminate the contract and that it would be best to assess the consequences of the breach, as quoted by Diplock LJ "the nature of the event to which the breach gives rise". Using the above we can suggest that while the breach of the term relating to Sir George Ditcher may be detrimental to Boris, the fundamental contract remains as in its standard form, that is, to purchase a bi-plane from the First World War.

6. Identify potential claim / conclusion

Using this paper to first confirm that there is an implied term within the contract of sale, we can see that identifying the term as either a condition or a warranty, in its traditional sense, may be difficult. However the underlying fact is that Boris has purchased an asset of value, albeit above the market value of a First World War bi-plane, and that to maintain a contract between the parties it would be logical that the term be considered a warranty and that Boris be able to claim damages.

Chapter 10 Exclusion Clauses

Exemption Clauses

A clause which seeks to exclude all liability for certain breaches, that would otherwise have been implied is called an exclusion clause and a limitation clause similarly seeks to limit liability for any breach of such a term. Moreover, the term, 'exemption clause' is used to cover both limitation and exclusion clauses. As a rule of thumb the exclusion clause completely excludes liability whereas the limitation clause only seeks to limit liability to a specific sum. The general rule is that the parties are free to determine the terms of their own contract, but the courts and Parliament do not look favourably on exclusion clauses and have found various ways of limiting their effect.

Question and Answers

- Unfair Contract Terms Act 1979 Essay
- Exclusion Clause Problem Question

Unfair Contract Terms Act 1979 Essay

Question

What, if any, are the differences in scope between the Unfair Contract Terms Act 1977 and the Unfair Terms in Consumer Contracts Regulations 1999?

Answer

To fully answer this question we need first to look at the nature of exclusion clauses and the history behind this legislation. It is commonplace for a party drawing up a contract to seek to minimise the amount of liability that may be incurred in the performance of that contract. Contractual clauses that have this effect are usually called "exclusion clauses" or "limitation clauses". Exclusion clauses often attempt to exclude or limit liability for losses arising out of breach of contract, or for extra-contractual liabilities. Extra-contractual liabilities will often include losses for misrepresentation, or negligence in performing the contract.

On the one hand from a business point of view this limit on liability does make sound business sense. It could even be argued that it is logical for the consumer as well, say for example the provider of a service that is ineffective has to pay compensation for all the losses that arise from running a poor service, that cost will simply be passed on to the consumer. Nonetheless whatever the advantages of this argument, there are clearly exclusions that perpetuate an injustice so great that they can't be tolerated in a decent society. The archetypal case of this sort is Thompson v London Midland and Scottish Railway (1930)1. In this case, an elderly, illiterate woman bought a railway ticket which contained a reference to the railway company's standard terms and conditions. These included a statement that the railway would not accept liability for negligence. During the alighting of the train Mrs Thompson fell and broke her leg. When she sued the railway in negligence, the exclusion clause was upheld, to the amazement of almost everybody. Mrs Thompson was an adult of full capacity, despite being unable to read, and had the notional freedom to either enter the contact or refrain. The courts had begun to develop common-law rules that helped exclusion clauses to be brought under control, however, cases like this made it clear that some sort of control was required.

When the Unfair Contract Terms Act (1977) ('UCTA') was drafted, it tried to balance freedom of contract (the long established principle that adults of full capacity who make contracts with each other should abide by them) against the need to prevent injustice. The UCTA deals with a limited set of precise types of exclusion, only exemption clauses. For example, it strikes out any attempt disclaim liability for death or injury, and this would probably have allowed Mrs Thompson to win her case. Efforts to disclaim liability for losses caused by negligence will be struck out if they don't pass the test of "reasonableness". Another main point is that the UTCA restricts those who wish to exclude liability for selling poor-quality, defective goods, or goods that the seller doesn't have a right to sell, say if they are stolen. Finally, it makes attempts to exclude liability for misrepresentation subject to a test of reasonableness. Whereas so far we have only looked at the English Law, at the same time the EC was also looking at legislation to control these types of clauses. This is how the Unfair Terms in Consumer Contracts Regulations 19992, however these two pieces of legislation have a number of important differences.

First, UTCCR only benefits with consumers whereas anyone can benefit under the 1977 act but there is most protection for consumers. For the UTCCR purposes, a consumer is any "natural person" acting outside the course of his business. In fact, s.3 of the Regulation defines "consumer" as meaning (only) "any natural person who [...] is acting for purposes which are outside his trade, business or profession". The very narrow phrase "natural person" implies that only individuals will benefit from UTCCR, whereas under UCTA businesses can trade as consumers if outside of their course of business. However although the UCTA 1977 introduced for the very first time the distinction between "consumer and "non consumer" the very definition of "consumer" in the UCTA leaves

106

a lot to the interpretation the judges, so here we see the difference between the 1977 Act and the 1999 Regulations. In most instances it is not necessarily obvious what a consumer is and isn't, in a number of borderline situations. For example the case of **R and B Customs Brokers v UDT** the Court of Appeal held that a family firm that bought a car, partly for work and partly for social use, was a consumer for the purposes of UCTA. It isn't necessarily obvious what a consumer may be, in a number of borderline situations. Thus in **R and B Customs Brokers** would be excluded, unless they claimed as private individuals. There is, therefore, a difference between a `consumer' for UCTA purposes and for UTCCR purposes. There would, no doubt, be a large number of cases in which whether a person was a `consumer' or not would be decided the same way for both UCTA and UTCCR; but there are cases where it wouldn't. For example, in UCTA a person who buys at auction is, by definition, not a consumer. However, there is nothing in UTCCR that prevents a private individual buying at auction being a consumer.

So a second important difference is that the UTCCR deals not only with exclusion clauses, but any "unfair" term. The UCTA has a delicate balancing act to perform, that it only deals with exclusion clauses, and these are only one type of onerous contractual clause that causes problems. Consider the infamous case of **Interfoto v Stiletto** (1989). Here an advertising agency asked a photographic service to produce photographs for a presentation. The photographic service sent 47 transparencies to the agency for inspection, along with a contractual letter which had in its small print the statement that transparencies were to be returned within 14 days. If they were not, the service would levy a charge of £5 per negative per day. The agency forgot about the transparencies for a couple of weeks, and was rather surprised to receive a bill for £3,783. The Court of Appeal held that a term as onerous as this would have to be made very clear if it was to be enforced and the claimants had not done anything to bring it to the defendant's attention. As a result, the claim failed. This process of striking out a clause on the grounds of incomplete "incorporation" was one of the ways that the courts had sought to control exclusion clauses in the pre-UCTA days. While the Interfoto case showed that the

107

courts were prepared to go through the whole process again for other types of onerous clause, this was hardly satisfactory.

In the UTCCR the possibilities of "unfair terms" come to light. An unfair term is any that imbalances rights and obligations significantly to the detriment of the consumer. Like UCTA's notion of "reasonableness", "unfair" is not defined, but there is guidance. For example, a clause might be unfair if it allows the business to terminate the contract at its discretion, without extending the same freedom to the consumer. Another example is a term allowing the business to vary the contract without the consent of the consumer. This idea of "unfairness" goes much further than UCTA's "unreasonableness". The UCTA does not prevent a contract containing terms that allow one party to vary its obligations, for example. However, UTCCR does nothing to control onerous terms in non-consumer contracts. This means that the defendants in the Interfoto case would not be able to rely on UTCCR to escape their bill. It still falls to the courts to handle situations like this on a case-by-case basis.

Third, UTCCR applies only to terms that have not been individually negotiated between the parties. A term that has been influenced by the consumer is, by definition, fair. UCTA does not define what it means to be reasonable, but it does give some guidance. Under the UCTA, the test of reasonableness does allow for consideration of whether the term was negotiated, but this is only advisory. A negotiated term can still be deemed unreasonable. The courts are to have regard for, among other things, the relative bargaining positions of the parties, whether the contract is negotiated or in standard form, and whether the party affected by the exclusion clause was offered an incentive to contract on particular terms. This approach allows the courts a lot of flexibility, and some surprisingly draconian exclusion clauses have been upheld. For example, in **SAM Business Systems v Hedley and Co** a software supplier was allowed to rely on an exclusion clause that allowed it to supply a thoroughly inadequate product. The court decided that the parties were of roughly equal bargaining power, and the purchasers could have attempted to negotiate better terms. The court also recognised that such clauses are ubiquitous in the computing industry. Had the purchaser been a consumer, the reasonableness test would not have applied; the exclusion clause would simply have been struck out, because it attempted to disclaim liability for supplying goods that are not suitable for their purpose.

Fourth the explanation of "unfairness" in UTCCR includes the phrase "contrary to the requirements of good faith". This seems be tricky as it implies that the drafter of a consumer contract has an obligation to contract in good faith. In English law we do not officially recognise the doctrine of good faith as other countries do. However, UTCCR comes from the EC, and the idea of contractual good faith is less unusual in other parts of Europe. There are very few cases which consider what "good faith" actually is in terms of consumer contracts, so it may be that this phrase adds little to our understanding of unfairness.

So there are clearly two major pieces of legislation that overlap, but not totally. Certain contractual arrangements are caught by both UCTA and UTCCR and handled the same. For example, both UCTA (certainly) and UTCCR (advisedly) would strike out a clause that attempted to disclaim liability for death or injury of a party. Situations like this should not cause any problems. Then there are contractual arrangements that are handled by one of the pieces of legislation and not the other. For example, UTCCR deals with onerous terms in consumer contracts, while these are beyond the remit of UCTA. Some contractual arrangements are within the scope of both UCTA and UTCCR, but are subject to different tests. For example, consider a term in a contract for supply of goods and services that tried to disclaim liability for faulty goods where the manufacturers were to blame for the faults. Such a term would be void under UCTA if the purchaser were a consumer, void unless reasonable under UCTA if the purchaser were a business, void if `unfair' under UTCCR if the purchaser is a consumer, and unaffected by UTCCR if the purchaser is a business. Since `unfair' is not the same as `unreasonable', these complications are even more opaque. Finally, some contractual injustices that cry out for redress are handled neither by UCTA nor UTCCR. For example, a large, powerful business can still

109

impose onerous terms on a small business, and there is no statutory protection against these terms.

Aside from the problems of understanding which types of term in which strain of contract are caught by which piece of legislation, there is the additional problem that UTCCR goes beyond striking out unfair terms: it also establishes certain obligations on the contract those who draught contracts, to write in clear language. This may be no bad thing, but there is no similar rule for business contracts. To conclude, the law on statutory control of exclusion clauses is in a deplorable phase. Perhaps there needs to be a reassessment of this legislation to unify the UCTA and the UTCCR. More specifically, to amalgamate the rules corresponding to businesses and consumers and to supersede the "fairness" and "reasonable" tests with a common test to apply to all types of contract.

Exclusion Clause Problem Question

Question

Kate parks her new sports car in Wood Lane private car park. When she entered the car park, she paid for her parking. Consequently, she has affixes a ticket to her window. When she returns to her car, she discovers that her car has been seriously dented.

She complains to the management of Wood Lane private car park about the damage to the car. The management, while sympathetic, point out the terms and conditions on the back of the ticket which state that "management is not responsible for any damage" and that "cars are parked at owners' risk".

Discuss the validity of the exclusion/exemption clause in the terms and conditions of the ticket at Wood Lane private car park.

Answer

Introduction

This paper will first discuss the liability that has arisen. Second it will discuss the incorporation of the exclusion clause. It will then discuss construction of the exclusion clause. It will then discuss statutory controls such as the Unfair Contract Terms Act 1977.

Liability

Kate parks her new sports car in Wood Lane private car park. When she entered the car park, she paid for her parking. Consequently, she affixed a ticket to her window. When she returns to her car, she discovers that her car has been seriously dented. It is not clear from the question, by whom the dent has been caused by. If it has been caused by an employee or agent of the garage the garage will be liable for negligence that has caused damage.

111

Bailment is a temporary transfer of property to another for a limited time and for a specific purpose. The transfer of property in a bailment is only in regards to possession, not ownership. For cars, you turn over possession and care over to the lot, for example by giving a valet your car key. If you store your car in a lot for a prolonged period, but you maintain possession by keeping the keys or you pay a fee to park and retrieve your car on your own, you are likely not in a bailment situation.

If you are in a bailment situation, the lot owner has a duty to exercise reasonable care in safeguarding your vehicle. The owner would be liable if your windshield gets broken, someone crashes your car, some steals your car, or someone breaks into your car and the lot owner was not exercising reasonable care. For example, the lot owner cannot leave the keys in car and then not guard the car at all or leave windows open.

Incorporation of Exclusion Clause

Clearly no exclusion clause is valid if it is not part of the contract, and it is not part of the contract unless both parties agreed to it at the time. There are three ways in which an exclusion clause can become incorporated into the contract: signature, reasonable notice and pervious course of dealings.

Signature

The first way this can happen is through signature. This is demonstrated in the case of **L'Estrange v Graucob**[219] in which the court stated that in the absence of misrepresentation, where a party signs a document they will normally be bound by its contents whether or not he has read them. In the absence of misrepresentation, a party who signs a document is normally bound by its contents whether or not they have read them.

Reasonable Notice

The other way in which a term can become incorporated id

---

[219] [1934] 2 KB 394

through reasonable notice. Whether the term has become incorporated through this method will depend on the timing of any notice, the form it took and its effect. In respect of timing Kate has seen signs on Cheryl's premises which state. Kate has never requested sight of the terms and conditions. This would suggest it was brought to her attention before the contact was signed. This is essentially what the court is looking for and it has been demonstrated by many cases.[220] Secondly the form of the document that contains the clause must be a contractual document and not a receipt or note.[221] This appears to be satisfied. Lastly the effect of the clause is a determining factor. Lord Denning MR has famously said that the more onerous the clause, the better notice of it needed to be given. He went on to say: "In order to give sufficient notice, it would need to be printed in red ink with a red hand pointing to it - or something equally startling."[222] It appears that in the circumstances the court will agree incorporation has taken place through reasonable notice, although more information is needed to say for certain.

Previous Course of Dealings

The terms and condition will have most certainly been incorporated into this contract through the doctrine of previous course of dealings. The authority for this is the case of **Spurling Ltd v Bradshaw**[223] in which Denning, Morris and Parker LJ held that although the warehouse employees were negligent; their exclusion clause effectively exempted them as it had become incorporated as the two parties had traded on the same terms previously.

Contra proferentem

Any ambiguity or uncertainty in the interpretation of an exclusion clause, however contrived the ambiguity might be, is normally construed *contra proferentem* - against the party seeking to rely

---

[220]*Thornton v Shoe Lane*Parking Ltd [1971] 2 QB 163; and *Olley v Marlborough Court Hotel*[1949] 1 KB 532
[221]**Chapelton v Barry Urban District Council** [1940] 1 KB 532
[222]**Thornton v Shoe Lane Parking Ltd** [1971] 2 QB 163 at 170
[223] [1956] EWCA Civ 3

113

on it. In **White v Warwick** [1953] 2 All ER 1021, the plaintiff hired a bicycle from the defendant under a written agreement which included a provision that "nothing in this agreement shall render the owners liable for any personal injuries". the plaintiff was injured when the saddle tilted forward, and the Court of Appeal found the defendant liable in negligence. The exclusion clause was construed so as to exclude only the concurrent liability that would otherwise have arisen under the contract. The plaintiff was able then to sue in tort.

Statutory Control

Various statutory provisions invalidate or limit purported exclusion clauses. The most important parts of the *Unfair Contract Terms Act 1977* (which in spite of its name applies to tort as well as contract), apply only to business liability. It deals with both exclusion and limitation clauses, including those which impose restrictive conditions such as clauses which deny liability unless notice of any complaint is given within a specified time.

Much of the Act is concerned with the protection of consumers, and a consumer is defined in s.12 as amended as a legal person who does not make the contract in the course of business, nor purport to do so, while the other party does. In the case of an individual that is enough; where the buyer is a corporate body the goods must be of a type normally supplied for private consumption. The definition excludes a person (even an individual) buying second-hand goods at public auction, as well as a person who obtains goods (even for private use) by using a cash-and-carry card at a wholesale warehouse.

In **R & B Customs Brokers v UDT** [1988] 1 All ER 847, the plaintiff bought a car from a finance company the defendant, and the contract excluded any implied conditions as to the car's fitness in relation to any business transaction. The car proved to be faulty, and the plaintiff sued. The Court of Appeal said that where a transaction is only incidental to a business activity, a degree of regularity is needed before the transaction can be said to be "in the course of business". The plaintiff who was buying a car for only the second or third time was entitled to be regarded as consumers. Kate will be deemed a consumer.

Under section 2(2) Unfair Contract Terms Act 1977. The garages exclusion of liability will only be valid if it satisfies the test of reasonableness as contained in section 11 of Unfair Contract Terms Act 1977.The reasonableness test is contained at s.11 of UCTA and refers you to the matters specified in schedule 2, where there are 5 guidelines for the application of the reasonableness test:

The first guideline is equality and the strength of the bargaining positions of the parties. Are the parties relative to one another? The leading case on this point is **St Alban's City and District Council v ICL** where the crucial factor in deciding an exemption clause was not reasonable was that ICL was a massive computer company dealing with a small local council. The second is choice i.e. whether the customer received an inducement to agree to the term or had the opportunity to enter a similar contract with other persons but without a similar clause. Did the customer have any choice than to deal with this company? In **St Alban's** there was no choice as the software was not available anywhere else. This guideline also talks about inducements as in **Woodman v Photo Trade Processing**. The third is knowledge, i.e. whether the buyer knew the existence and extent of the term. The fourth guideline is time and the last is whether the goods were manufactured, processed or adapted to the special order of the customer.

Chapter 11 Misrepresentation

Misrepresentation

Jill Poole states an actionable misrepresentation to be: an unambiguous, false, statement of fact (or law), addressed to the party misled, which is material and induces the contract, and causes loss.[224] Any pre-contractual statements made by the parties during negotiations can be referred to as **'representations'**. 'Representations' are statements of fact (or law) and any false statement of fact is a **'misrepresentation'**. If the untrue statement of fact made by one party has been relied on by another party before entering into the contract, it renders the contract voidable.

Question and Answer

- Misrepresentation Problem Question

---

[224]Poole, Jill. *Textbook on contractlaw*. Oxford UniversityPress, 2012.

Misrepresentation Problem Question

Question

Jack is considering buying his aunt Jess's house as an investment. During the negotiations, Jess states, "This house is worth £200,000 and I've had two separate valuations from estate agents verifying that, but since I love you so much I'll sell it to you for £180,000." Jess has not received any valuations from estate agents and the house is worth only £120,000. Jack buys the house for £180,000. Two weeks after Jack has completed the sale and moved into the house, he discovers that Jess did not receive any valuations from estate agents. The same week, Jack discovers that the value of the house has been reduced to £80,000 due to serious damage caused by the collapse of a supporting wall. At this point, a buyer offers £80,000 for the house. Jack does not sell the house until three months later, when Jack only receives £75,000 for the house because of a general fall of the property market.

Advise Jack.

Answer

Introduction

This is an advice for Jack regarding the purchase of his Aunt Jess's house. It will discuss whether the contract can be set aside on grounds of misrepresentation, rather than on grounds of breach of contract. This advice will thus discusses the following: whether misrepresentation is established, the type of misrepresentation, the remedies available to Jack and the summary of advice.

Term or representation

Jack's aunt Jess during the pre-contract negotiations made several statements, the main one being: *"I've had two separate valuations from estate agents"*. The second was the value of the house was *"worth £200,000"*. The third being silent about the defective wall. The latter two statements stem from the first that a valuation had been carried out. If in fact a valuation had been carried out it would have given Jack a clear indication of i) the value of the house; ii) and the condition of the house, thus exposing any defects. Would these statements have become terms? This is quite possibly. But the expected market value did not appear on the contact; neither did any defects or the soundness of the house. Therefore this advice advises on the assumption that the aunt's statements are representations, the following advice thus discusses whether these representation are actionable misrepresentations.

The misrepresentation

The following statement of Jess gives rise to a potential claim for misrepresentation: *"This house is worth £200,000 and I've had two separate valuations from estate agents verifying that"*. Poole defines an actionable misrepresentation as: *"an unambiguous, false, statement of fact made to the claimant, which induces the claimant to enter into the contract with the statement maker."*[225]If the above elements are established Jack may have an arguable case for misrepresentation which can make the contract voidable.

Unambiguous statement

The statements made by Jess about both the existence of valuations and the market value of the house was unambiguous and did not lend itself to misinterpretation on the part of Jack. In order to form the basis of a claim the representation must indeed be clear, keeping in mind that the representor may not be liable on the grounds that the representee unreasonably interpreted it. In **McInerny v Lloyds Bank Ltd**[226]the Court of Appeal held that the representor may not be liable when the representee misconstrues the representation[227]. Here Jack has believed Jess in what she is saying and not unreasonably constructed neither the value of the house or the fact that a valuation has been carried out. He has been categorically been told this.

---

[225]Poole, Jill. *Textbook on contract law.* Oxford University Press, 2012, at 515
[226](1974) 1 Lloyd's Rep 246
[227] McInerny v Lloyd's Bank Ltd [1974] 1 Lloyd's Rep 246

False Statement

Jack discovers that Jess did not receive any valuations from estate agents. To be actionable misrepresentation the representation must be substantially false, as opposed to substantially correct. In **Avon Insurance Plc v Swire Fraser Ltd**[228], Rix J stated: *"[A] representation may be true without being entirely correct, provided it is substantially correct and the difference between what is represented and what is actually correct would not have been likely to induce a reasonable person in the position of the claimants to enter into the contracts"*. Therefore Jess saying the valuations existed to justify the market value of £200,000 was a false statement which ultimately induced Jack

Statement of existing fact

Poole explains that to be actionable, a representation must be a statement of fact. Factual statements have to be distinguished from statements which are not actionable such as: statements of opinion, future intention as well as instances of silence.[229]

A statement of opinion

Although a statement of opinion is not a statement of fact, it may be considered a statement of fact if it is proved that the representor did not believe in it or if a reasonable man with the knowledge of the representor would not have held. In **Smith v Land and House Property Corporation**,[230] Bowen LJ held:

> *"Where the facts are equally well known to both parties, what one of them says to the other is frequently nothing but an expression of opinion…But if the facts are not equally known to both sides, then a statement of opinion by the one who knows the facts*

---

[228] (2000) 1 All ER (Comm) 573
[229] Poole, Jill. Textbook on contract law. Oxford University Press, 2012. 523
[230] (1884) 28 ChD 7 (CA)

best involves very often a statement of material fact, for he impliedly states that he knows the facts that justifies his opinion."

As Jess said the house was worth £200,000 she could argue that this was merely her opinion. But using the above authority, Jack can argue that since her opinion was backed by the fact there was a valuation to verify this. She is saying she has the expert opinion of a valuation; this makes the statement one of fact rather than opinion.

Statement of valuation and silence about the wall

Jess's false statement about the existence of a valuation leads to the non-disclosure of the defect in the wall. These are linked. Indeed, if a valuation was carried out, it would have informed Jack about the state of the wall and certainly factored it into the evaluation of the market price of the house. As a result, the value of the house has been reduced to £80,000 due to serious damage caused by the collapse of a supporting wall, Jack may argue that Jess's lack of disclosure about the state of the wall at the time of the negotiations amounts to silence, which may be considered a misrepresentation under the circumstances at hand.

Silence does not generally amount to misrepresentation, according to the principle of *caveat emptor*. Thus a claim on the ground of misrepresentation may not be based on it. The case **Keates v The Earl of Cadogan**[231] defines this area of law. The Court established the principle that there is no general duty of disclosure and that it is justified that such a general duty would lack precision as it would not be possible to define which facts would have to be disclosed in advance. Thus Jess has no general duty to disclose facts that may impact Jack's willingness to enter into the contract. The case **Sykes v Taylor-Rose**[232] further establishes that the courts will assess what duty of disclosure exists on a case by case basis.

---

[231] (1851) 10 CB 591
[232] [2004] EWCA Civ 299

However, one line of argument that Jess and her lawyer may attempt to use is that a valuation was being sought, however did not happen in time. As we will see later, this is the only way she can show she had reasonable belief in the statement (an argument she will have to make when arguing remedy). If the court accepts a valuation was sought then at the beginning of negotiations, where a statement is made which is true but which, prior to entering into the contract becomes false, the representor is under an obligation to correct the representation. If Jess then fails to inform Jack that no valuation has been done and allows Jack to enter into the contract still believing that a valuation has been carried out then she will be liable for misrepresentation.

In **With v O'Flanagan**[233] a man selling his medical practice stated at the beginning of the negotiation that it was worth a certain price. During the course of the negotiations the price fell dramatically and the man did not inform the buyer of that fact. The court ruled that by his silence about the change of price he had made an ongoing representation[234].

Using the above authority the fact that Jess has not told Jack that there is no valuation and this is inconstant with the obligation where a continuing representation is made which becomes false. The same applies to the valuation where one did not materialise at the time of sale. Indeed, had the valuations happened, the defect in the wall would have been exposed. It may be Jess already knowns about the defect in the wall, but remaining silent about it does not constitute actionable misrepresentation because the duty of disclosure does not extend to physical defects in the property itself. It may be that the loss of value to the house because of the wall could still be recoverable as it stems from the misrepresentation about the valuation.

Statement addressed to the party misled

---

[233] [1936] Ch 575
[234] Bigwood, R. (2005). PRE-CONTRACTUAL MISREPRESENTATION AND THE LIMITS OF THE PRINCIPLE IN WITH V. O'FLANAGAN. *The Cambridge Law Journal*, 64(01), 94-125.

Jess and Jack negotiated the contract face to face and Jack is thus aware of the representation. For the misrepresentation to be actionable, the representation must be addressed to the party misled. The authority for the law is the case **Peek v Gurney**[235]. It is thus established that Jess addressed her statements to Jack.

Statement inducing the contract

In order to be actionable misrepresentation, the representation must have been at least one of the reasons Jack entered into the contract. The authority on the law is the case is **Edgington v Fitzmaurice**[236]. Jack was induced into entering into the contract and paid the stated price for the house because Jess had stated that the valuations had taken place and that in turn the price of the house was validated by expert opinion. There was no other inducement.

If Jess wishes to prove that Jack bought the house independent of her representation, the burden of proof is on her to disprove Jack's claim. Indeed, the representor has to prove that the representee did not rely on the representation to enter the contract, according to **Peekay Intermark Ltd & Anor v Australia & New Zealand Banking Group Ltd**[237] (2006). Based on the facts of the case it is unlikely that Jess would successfully prove that her representation was immaterial in Jack's decision to enter into the contract. As we will now discuss, had Jack conducted his own valuation of the house Jess chances to dismiss Jack's claim would have been greater.

Opportunity to discover the truth

Jack could have carried out his own independent valuation about the house, yet he did not, relying instead on Jess statement about valuations. The case of **Attwood v Small**[238] establishes the principle that when a representee conducts his own independent

---

[235] (1873) LR 6 HL 377
[236] (1885) 29 Ch D 459
[237] (2006) EWCA Civ 386
[238] (1838) 6 CL & F 232

investigation about the representation, he will no longer be considered to have relied on it but instead on his own analysis. Since Jack did not conduct independent valuation of the house, Jess may not claim that Jack relied on his own judgement.

Moreover, the fact that Jack did not conduct his own investigation does not render his reliance on the representation immaterial. The case **Redgrave v Hurd**[239], establishes that are presentee has no obligation to verify the statement of the representor and that he may have relied on the misrepresentation to enter the contract. In addition, the case, **Smith v Eric S. Bush**[240], details the law, specifying that the more commercially aware are presentee is the more it is expected that he investigates the representation and conversely, the least commercially aware the representee is the less he is expected to investigate the representation. Thus we can conclude using the authorities above that as this not a commercial transaction and Jack was private buyer purchasing the house from his Aunt he had no duty to conduct own investigations. In addition, it would be reasonable for Jack to have trusted his aunty. Then again this is the sale of a house as an investment worth £200,000 and this size of investment warrants a valuation through survey in our current volatile housing market. Although any solicitor conducting Jack conveyance would insist on an independent valuation, this advice nevertheless considers there was no duty on Jack to carry out a valuation.

The type of misrepresentation

We must now consider the type of misrepresentation that has occurred, because this will have an effect of the outcome of the remedy available.

Fraudulent misrepresentation was articulated by Lord Herschell in the House of Lords when he decided the case **Derry v Peek**[241] and defined fraud as follows:

---

[239] (1881) 20 Ch D1
[240] (1990) 1 AC 831
[241] (1889) LR14 App Cas 337

> "...it must be shown that a false representation was made (a) knowingly, or (b) without belief in its truth, or (c) recklessly, careless whether it be true or false."

The burden of proof is on the representee to establish that the elements above are present that is that the representor knew his statement was not true, or did not believe it was true or was reckless about its truth. As we do not know what Jess's state of mind was when she said *"this house is worth £200,000 and I've had two separate valuations from estate agents verifying that..."* it is unlikely that fraudulent misrepresentation may be established. The facts provided do not appear sufficient to base a claim on the tort of deceit.

Section 2(1) of the Misrepresentation Act 1967[242] provides:

> "Where a person has entered into a contract after a misrepresentation has been made to him by another party thereto and as a result thereof he has suffered loss, then, if the person making the misrepresentation would be liable to damages in respect thereof had the misrepresentation been made fraudulently, that person shall be so liable notwithstanding that the misrepresentation was not made fraudulently, unless he proves that he had reasonable grounds to believe and did believe up to the time the contract was made that the facts represented were true."

According to the definition of a negligent misrepresentation above, a negligent misrepresentation is a misrepresentation which Jess may believe but has no "reasonable grounds to believe." Also, the case **Howard Marine & Dredging Co. Ltd v A. Ogden & Sons (Excavations) Ltd**[243] further details that at the defendant must substantiate his beliefs. According to the authorities above the burden of proof moves to Jess to prove that her belief the house was worth £200,000 was grounded on serious evidence[244]. If she

---

[242] Section 2(1)Misrepresentation Act 1967
[243] (1978) QB 574
[244] Sealy, L. S. (1978). Contract—Damages for Misrepresentation. *The Cambridge Law*

proves this the misrepresentation will be deemed innocent misrepresentation, according to **Thomas Witter Ltd v TBP Industries Ltd**[245]. To conclude it is likely on a balance of probabilities that the misrepresentation will be negligent because on the papers there is no reason offered for her false statement. Also, where Jess is found liable for a negligent misrepresentation under S(2), Jack will be able to claim the same level of damages as if it the misrepresentation had been fraudulent. Indeed, the case **Royscott Trust Ltd v Rogerson**[246] confirms that liability in damages cover all losses consequential to the misrepresentation. Based on the above elements, this advice recommends that Jack bases his claim on s.(2) of the Misrepresentation Act 1967.

The remedy

According to Poole, the effect of misrepresentation is to render the contract voidable but not void and rescission is available for misrepresentation under the Section 2(2) and generally, rescission will be awarded only where the parties can be restored to their original position by returning all the property transferred between the parties under the contract.[247] As there has been negligent misrepresentation, Jack would have been entitled to rescind the contract with Jess.

However, this option is not available to Jack for he has sold the house for £75,000 and according to **Clarke v Dickson**[248] this prevents him and Jess to be restored to their original pre-contract positions.

Thus Jack can only claim damages, under Section 2(2) of the Misrepresentation Act 1967. Damages for fraudulent misrepresentation are potentially the greatest available for misrepresentation. However, it must be borne in mind that an action for negligent misrepresentation, under s2(1) MA 1967, will often match those that would be available for fraudulent

---

Journal, 37(02), 229-232.
[245] (1996) 2 All ER 573
[246] (1991) 2 QB 297
[247] Poole, Jill. *Textbook on contract law*, Oxford University Press, 2012, at 536
[248] (1858) EB & E 148

misrepresentation, if Jess cannot prove she had reasonable belief in the statement.

The damages that are recoverable are everything that stems from the misrepresentation. According to **William Sindall plc v Cambridgeshire County Council**[249] liability for damages under section 2(2) are interpreted as meaning *"the difference in value between what the claimant was misled into believing he was acquiring and the value of what he in fact received."* Jack starting cost was £180,000. He cannot recover what he was told the house was worth because he did not pay this amount (£200,000). He cannot recover loss of profit (£20,000) because it does not stem from the misrepresentation. He can arguably recover for the loss of £40,000 because the wall collapsed and this was the decrease in value, and as this was a direct result of the misstatement about the valuation which would have informed him of the wall and the state of the house. If he knew about the true value and the defect he would probably not have entered into this contract. The shortfall of £5,000 will not be recoverable as this is attributable to the market forces and not the misrepresentation. Therefore, the total he will recoup is £75,000 from the sale of the house plus £40,000 due to the collapse of the wall. This amounts to £115,000. Thus he has made a loss of £65,000.

Summary of advice

The advice proposes that Jack places a claim for damages for misrepresentation under Section 2(1) of the Misrepresentation Act 1967. If the courts find that the misrepresentation is material, Jack may be awarded the damages flowing from the misrepresentation that is £40,000.

---

[249] (1994) 1 WLR 1016

Chapter 12 Mistake

Mistake

Various mistakes may occur in the negotiations leading to the formation of a contract, and they are not all treated the same. We distinguish three kinds of mistake, though different writers use different names and different classifications. A common mistake, we shall say, occurs when both parties make the same mistake (eg as to the existence, ownership or nature of the subject-matter of the contract). A mutual mistake occurs when each party is mistaken as to the intentions of the other in respect of the contract, and a unilateral mistake occurs when just one party is mistaken as to the identity or intention of the other, or as to the nature of a document being signed. A mistake renders a contract void.

Question and Answer

- Mistake Problem Question

Mistake Problem Question

Question

Assume that Skywards Ltd are granted planning permission to build their office block. As the block promises to be the tallest building in Manchester, it receives much local press coverage.

Irmina, a supplier of building materials, is contacted by Michael, who introduces himself as the chairman of ReachSkywards Ltd. Michael tells Irmina that his company needs to place a large order for various building materials, but that, until financing arrangements are concluded, this will have to be on credit. Irmina mistakenly believes that ReachSkywards is the company she has read about in the local papers, who are building the tallest office block in Manchester. As such, she thinks that there is little risk in allowing Michael to have credit. Consequently, they enter into a contract, and Michael takes delivery of the materials. Payment is to be made a month later. However, Michael does not pay. When Irmina, by now quite worried, tries to contact Michael she discovers her mistake. She phones Michael, who tells her, "too bad – sue us if you like, but there is a long list of creditors ahead of you! Those materials are ours now."

Advise Irmina (ignoring any issue of criminal liability).

Answer

Introduction

This paper advises Irmina on her position in relation to her agreement with Reachskywards Limited. The most desirable option for Irmina would be to put forward a successful argument to the effect that her mistake as to Michael's identity negatives her consent to the contract, rendering the contract void *ab initio*. This would allow Irmina to obtain the return of her goods from Michael. This paper will therefore examine the case law in this area in order to determine whether it is advisable for Irmina to pursue such an argument. This paper will then put forward the remedies available to Irmina as a result of Michael breaching the contract.

Mistaken Identity

Where there is a genuine mistake as to the identity of one of the contracting parties, and this mistake is of fundamental importance, the mistake will render the contract void *ab initio*.[250] Should Irmina be able to show that her mistake, in thinking that Michael from Reachskywards Limited was in fact from Skywards Ltd, was of fundamental importance to her entering into the contract then she may be able to succeed in such an argument.

The most recent case involving mistaken identity **Shogun Finance Ltd v Hudson**[251] draws a distinction between contracts made *inter presentes* (face to face) and contracts made *inter absentes* (non-face to face, i.e. in writing). As it is not strictly clear from the facts provided in relation to the agreement between Irmina and Michael from Reachskywards Limited, how their contract was concluded, it is necessary to look at both scenarios in turn. This paper will then conclude having determined whether Irmina would succeed in such an argument.

The cases that will be examined all involve the goods being passed on to a third party, as it is not suggested that a third party is involved in Irmina's situation this paper will not examine this aspect of these cases.

Inter presentes

Where two parties enter into a contract *inter presents* the legal principle is that there is a *prima facie* presumption that the parties intend to contract with the person in front of them, notwithstanding the fact that there has been a mistake.[252] The burden of rebutting this presumption falls on the party claiming

---

[250] Catherine Elliot and Frances Quinn, Contract Law (7th edn, Pearson Education Limited 2009) 218
[251] [2004] 1 A.C. 919
[252] Michael Furmston, Cheshire, Fifoot&Furmston's Law of Contract (15th edn, Oxford University Press 2007) 310

that there has been a mistake.[253] As Irmina would therefore carry this burden it is necessary to consider her likelihood of success in rebutting the presumption.

In **Phillips v Brooks Limited**[254] and **Lewis v Averay**[255] the innocent parties were unsuccessful in rebutting the *prima facie* presumption that they had intended to deal with the person in front of them. The courts concluded that although they may have been mistaken as to the identity of the other party, this was not of fundamental importance. The mistake that both innocent parties had made was a mistake as to the attributes of the other parties, namely their creditworthiness, which was not enough to render a contract void *ab initio*.

In **Ingram v Little**[256] however, although the facts were very similar to **Phillips v Brooks Limited** and **Lewis v Averay**, the innocent party was successful in rebutting the *prima facie* presumption. The courts found that the identity of the other party was of fundamental importance to the Ingram sisters, as they only agreed to the contract after checking the identity of the other party. The contract was as a result rendered void *ab initio*.

The irreconcilable decisions reached in these *inter presentaes* cases that relate to very similar facts, made this area of law uncertain,[257] until they were considered in *Shogun Finance Ltd v Hudson*. Lord Nicholls and Lord Phillips of Worth Matravers both preferred the dissenting judgement of Devlin LJ in **Ingram v Little** which was in line with the decisions in **Phillips v Brooks Limited** and **Lewis v Averay,** and Lord Millet and Lord Walker went even further, being of the opinion that *Ingram v Little* had been wrongly decided.[258] As a result of the *obiter* in **Shogun Finance Ltd v Hudson** it is clear that *Ingram v Little* will not be followed. There is now certainty that the presumption that parties in *inter presentaes* cases intend to deal with the person in front of

---

[253] ibid
[254] [1919] 2 K.B. 243
[255] [1973] 1 W.L.R. 510
[256] [1961] 1 Q.B. 31
[257] Ewan Mckendrick, Contract Law (8th edn, Palgrave Macmillan Law Masters 2009) 58
[258] ibid

them is a strong presumption that will be very difficult to rebut, just as in **Phillips v Brooks Limited** and **Lewis v Averay**.

Therefore if the agreement between Irmina and Michael from Reachskywards Limited was made *inter praesentes* then it is likely that the court would find that Irmina had intended to contract with him, despite her mistake in thinking that he was from Skywards Limited. They would be unable to conclude that her mistake had been one as to identity, thus rendering the contract void *ab inito*. They would instead conclude that the mistake made by her was one as to his attributes, his creditworthiness, thus leaving the contract intact.

Inter absentes

Where two parties enter into a contract *inter absentes* the courts look to the construction of the written document(s) to determine whom the parties intended to contract with, the legal principle is that there is a presumption that the parties intended to contract with the persons named in writing.[259] Therefore if Irmina and Michael made their agreement in writing then her success in a mistaken identity argument would fall on whether the written communication contained the name of Reachskywards Limited or Skywards Limited. This can be seen from the cases of **Cunday v Lindsay**[260], **King's Norton Metal Co Ltd v Edridge, Merrett & Co Ltd**[261] and **Shogun Finance Ltd v Hudson**.

In **Cunday v Lindsay** a rogue by the name of Blenkarn wrote to Lindsay, purporting to be from a firm by the name of Blenkiron & Co who was known to Lindsay by reputation. The written communication contained the name Blenkiron & Co, as a result the court found that Lindsay had intended to contract with Blenkiron & Co. The court stated that Lindsay could not have intended to contract with the rogue Belnkarn as he was unknown to Lindsay and was not named in the written communication. As

---

[259] Janet O'Sullivan and Jonathan Hilliard, The Law of Contract (4th edn, Oxford University Press 2010) 57
[260] (1877-78) L.R. 3 App. Cas. 459
[261] (1897) 14 TLR 98

Blenkarn had induced Lindsay into entering into the contract by misrepresenting his identity, at the time of making the contract Blenkarn was aware of Lindsay's mistake. As a result the contract was found to be void *ab initio* for mistake, as Blenkiron & Co was not aware of the agreement.

An additional requirement for a mistaken identity argument to succeed is that there is an identifiable third party with whom there was an intention to contract with. In **King's Norton Metal Co Ltd v Edridge, Merrett & Co Ltd** a rogue named Wallis, had placed an order in writing to King's Norton, purporting to be from a company named Hallam & Co. This company was unknown to King's Norton prior to them receiving the order. In determining whom King's Norton had intended to contract with the court again looked to the construction of the written communication. The documents contained the name of Hallam & Co, as there was no separate entity known to King's Norton by that name the court found that they could not have intended to contract with anyone other than the person writing the letters to them. Therefore there was found to be a valid contract between King's Norton and the rogue Wallis, who had deceived them by use of a trading name rather than by pretending to be from another existing company known to them. The only mistake that had been made was a mistake as to the attributes of the other party, which was not enough to render the contract void *ab initio*.

In **Shogun Finance Ltd v Hudson** a rogue went into a car showroom purporting to be an individual by the name of Mr Patel, an individual worthy of credit, with him he had a driving licence to prove 'his' identity. The finance company ran a credit check on Mr Patel, satisfied he was worthy of credit they entered into the finance agreement with Mr Patel and allowed the rogue, whom they believed was Mr Patel, to take the vehicle. The court again looked to the construction of the written document and determined that the finance company had intended to contract with Mr Patel, who was named in the written document, and not the rogue. As a result the contract was found to be void *ab initio* for mistake, as Mr Patel was not aware of the agreement.

When applying these principles to the facts provided which relate to Irmina and Michael's agreement, it appears as though the written communication would contain the company name of Reachskywards Limited, rather than Skywards Limited. Michael introduced himself to Irmina as the chairman of Reachskywards Limited. Irmina mistakenly thought that this was the company that she read about in the local papers (Skywards Limited). However this was not as a result of a misrepresentation on the part of Michael and there is nothing to suggest that Michael would have been aware of Irmina's mistake. As a result Irmina would be unsuccessful in arguing that she had been mistaken as to the other party's identity. She would be found to have intended to contract with Reachskywards Limited, therefore a contract a valid contract would have been concluded between the parties. Her mistake would be deemed to be a mistake as to the attributes of Reachskywards Limited, their creditworthiness, which would leave the contract intact.

If however the facts were different and the written communication between Irmina and Michael contained the company name of Skywards Limited, as they are a separate entity known to Irmina, it would be very likely that the courts would concluded that Irmina had intended to contract with Skywards Limited and therefore the contract would be void *ab initio* for mistake, as Skywards Limited knew nothing of the agreement.

Breach of Contract

It can be deduced from the facts provided that a valid contract exists between Irmina and Michael. (Reachskywards Limited). On this basis, it is advisable for Irmina to make a claim for an action for an agreed sum as a result of the breach of contract.[262] It is unclear from the facts provided as to the exact terms agreed between the parties. Should Irmina have expressly incorporated a 'reservation of title' clause into the contract, which is common practice in the building trade, then she would instead be able to reclaim possession of the goods.[263]

---

[262] Elliot and Quinn, op.cit. 357
[263] P.S. Atiyah, John N. Adams and Hector Macqueen, The Sale of Goods (11[th]edn,

Pearson Longman 2005) 470

Chapter 13 Remedies

This chapter deals with remedies that are available to the aggrieved party when there is a breach of contract. Without a remedy, a right would be of no value. Many remedial responses when a breach of contract occurs have evolved over the years.

Question and Answers

- Remedies Problem Question

Remedies Problem Question

Question

Helen decided to set up a business as a potter. She entered into a contract with a local builder, Eric, to convert her shed into a potting studio, complete with wheel and kiln. The contract was for £15,000 and provided that the work would be finished by 30 June. However, Eric had problems with labour and did not complete the work until 30 September. Helen had to cancel a number of pottery jobs over the summer, including a lucrative contract for a dining set of her pottery in the restaurant at Lowclere, a local stately home and the sale of the pottery at Lowclere's gift shop. The cancellation of these jobs in the summer season has caused Helen significant mental distress.

Advise Helen.

Answer

Introduction

This essay will discuss the opportunity for Helen to obtain damages in the context of a local builder's delay in the delivery of her potting studio. The goal of her claim is for her to be in the position she would have been in had the contract been performed properly. We will discuss the following losses:

1. Cancelation of Pottery jobs at Lowclere gift shop
2. A lucrative contract for a dining set
3. Mental distress

Cancelation of Pottery jobs

We will discuss Helen's pecuniary loss in connection with the cancellation of pottery jobs at the gift shop. These are expectation loss. Using **Barries and Davis** as an authority, Helen may place a claim on the expected profits had the contract been properly performed. We now discuss the remoteness, mitigation and causation requirements. **Hadley v Baxendale** provides a test to assess the remoteness element of the claim. The claimant needs to establish that the loss naturally flew from the breach and that it was foreseeable that the loss would occur. As the builder is a local builder and was probably aware that Helen was running a pottery business and had ongoing contracts to provide local shops with her products we argue that is was foreseeable that she would incur some loss as a result of the delay. We argue that the loss naturally flew from the delay. **Quinn v Burch Brothers** establishes that the breach must be the cause of the loss. According to the facts the loss is caused by the delay. Finally, Brace v Calder establishes that the claimant has a duty to mitigate the loss. Thus Helen has to establish that she took steps to mitigate her loss. On the facts of the case we argue that there is not much she could do to mitigate the loss resulting from the delay. Thus Helen may place a claim for damages based on the loss of profits she would have realised had the pottery studio be ready on time.

Anglia TV provides that a claim for damages may be based on the investments incurred by the claimant in the context of the contract when losses are not materially measurable. Since Helen losses are measurable and the damage appears to be appropriate remedies to compensate Helen for her losses we do not advice Helen to place a claim for damages based on reliance.

Cancellation of a lucrative contract

We will discuss Helen's pecuniary loss in connection with the cancellation of a one-time pottery job for the restaurant. Using **Hadley v Baxendale** test, we argue that although the loss of this job resulted from the delay, it is debatable whether it was foreseeable that it would occur. Based on the facts, the builder may not have been aware of this specific contract. In **Victoria laundry** the courts held that only the loss of contemplated profits could be recoverable, but not the loss resulting from a cancelled contract which the defendant was not aware of. **Chaplin v Hicks** establishes that damages may be claim for loss of opportunity. We argue that Helen may claim that the contract for the restaurant constituted a chance for her to develop a new market segment of made-by-order pottery jobs and that the delay resulted in her missing that opportunity, even though the losses are speculative. Based on these authorities on the balance of probabilities we argue that Helen may not be able to claim damages for the loss of this specific contract.

Mental distress

We will discuss Helen's mental distress in connection with the builder's delay in setting up the pottery studio. This is non pecuniary loss occasioning distressed as defined in **Addis Gramophone** where the courts held that damages may not be claimed for mental distress. However, **Farley v Skinner** established that some compensation may be claimed if significant disturbance results from the loss. Jarvis v Swan tours established that damages may be claimed for distress if the object of the contract involves leisure and relaxation. On the fact Helen may not rely on this authority to place a claim since the contract does not pertain to a leisure activity.

We argue that besides the financial loss incurred Helen's distress is not material as she may not point to a specific disturbance, such as noise or the impossibility to use an item properly. Thus we argue that Helen may not claim damages for mental distress.

www.ingramcontent.com/pod-product-compliance
Ingram Content Group UK Ltd.
Pitfield, Milton Keynes, MK11 3LW, UK
UKHW051908181224
3751UKWH00058B/1048

Bass Jazz
A guide to left-hand technique

Featuring
50 Jazz Classics
for String Bass

by
ANDY McKEE

Cover photo: Paul Aresu

ISBN 978-1-4234-8953-5

7777 W. BLUEMOUND RD. P.O. BOX 13819 MILWAUKEE, WI 53213

Copyright © 2011 by HAL LEONARD CORPORATION
International Copyright Secured   All Rights Reserved

For all works contained herein:
Unauthorized copying, arranging, adapting, recording, Internet posting, public performance,
or other distribution of the printed music in this publication is an infringement of copyright.
Infringers are liable under the law.

Visit Hal Leonard Online at
www.halleonard.com

Contents

Endorsements ... iv
About the Author ... v
Acknowledgments ... vi
Introduction ... vii
Articulation Notes ... viii

Bye Bye Blackbird ... 1
Satin Doll ... 2
All of Me* ... 3
Autumn Leaves ... 4
Yesterdays ... 5
Blues in the Closet ... 6
Nardis ... 7
Don't Get Around Much Anymore* ... 8
Solar ... 9
Bass Blues ... 10
Softly as in a Morning Sunrise ... 11
Recorda-Me ... 12
Au Privave ... 13
Oleo* ... 14
Blue Skies ... 15
Scrapple from the Apple ... 16
Invitation ... 17
Doxy ... 18
Bohemia After Dark ... 19
Dig ... 20
Billie's Bounce (Bill's Bounce)* ... 21
A Night in Tunisia ... 22
Lullaby of Birdland ... 23
Goodbye Pork Pie Hat ... 24
Interplay ... 25
Lament* ... 26
Tail Feathers ... 27
Lester Left Town ... 28
In Walked Bud ... 29
Four ... 30
In a Sentimental Mood* ... 31
Well You Needn't (It's Over Now) ... 32
I Remember Clifford* ... 33
Israel ... 34
Ray's Idea ... 35
Afternoon in Paris ... 36
Epistrophy ... 37
Ornithology ... 38
Bloomdido ... 39
Pent Up House* ... 40
Receipt Please ... 41
Along Came Betty ... 42
Teen Town ... 43
Milestones ... 44
Girl from Ipanema (Garôta de Ipanema) ... 46
My One and Only Love* ... 47
Anthropology ... 48
Confirmation ... 49
Self-Portrait in Three Colors* ... 50
Moose the Mooche ... 51

*Arranged to be played arco.

Endorsements

"It is a wonderful idea for a book and will certainly be a useful tool in my studio!"

Associate Professor Lynn Seaton
University of North Texas
Denton, TX

"I am grateful that you are taking the time to do this. I feel it would be a *very* valuable addition to the literature, and would most certainly help developing jazz players devise much more logical fingering patterns for themselves."

Associate Professor Todd Coolman
Director of Jazz Studies
Purchase College-SUNY
Purchase, NY

"I really like the concept and think it will be a helpful and welcome addition to bass pedagogy."

John Clayton
University of Southern California
Irvine, CA

"Great work! You should definitely publish this stuff. My students love it."

Craig Thomas
University of the Arts
Philadelphia, PA

"Good job."

Professor Richard Davis
University of Wisconsin-Madison
Madison, WI

"This work is solid and sure to become the Simandl/Bille for the jazz bassist."

Jeff Carney
New School University
New York, NY

"*Bass on Top* offers a clear presentation of the left-hand techniques necessary to simulate swinging horn articulation. This book will help the student develop an excellent foundation for all musical situations in addition to the jazz idiom. I am looking forward to adding Andy's method book to our curriculum at New York University and Rutgers University."

Professor Mike Richmond
NYU Steinhardt School
New York, NY
Rutgers University
New Brunswick, NJ

"Andy McKee gives in this book very practical advice for a refined articulation of the jazz idiom on the double bass. Students as well as teachers will find here a very useful tool to get quick results for phrasing and expression on their instrument."

Riccardo Del Fra
Chair of Jazz and Improvised Music
Conservatoire National Supérieur de Musique et de Danse de Paris
Paris, France

About the Author

Whether you are talking about Andy McKee's bass playing or his way of moving through life, three words say it—strength, passion, and artistry. Performing for more than twenty-five years on the world's jazz stage, his reputation stretches from his home base of New York, across the United States, to Europe and Japan. The deep resonance of Andy's sound adds unmistakable dimension to every band he plays in. His impeccable time, musicianship, and capacity for rhythmic invention were forged over years of in-the-trenches experience with many legendary jazz masters.

Andy McKee is as comfortable on the concert stage as in the recording studio or jazz club. He has been a longtime member of the Mingus Big Band and the Mingus Dynasty as well as groups led by Elvin Jones, Michel Petrucciani, Chet Baker, and Philly Joe Jones. He has toured and recorded as a leader of his own group since 1995.

Throughout his career as a performing artist, Andy has recognized the great value in passing on the skills and insights gained through his years of study both on and off the bandstand. Inspired by students' passion for the music and their commitment to learning, Andy has always incorporated teaching into his professional life. He has been a faculty member at the New School University in New York City since 1993 and has conducted clinics and workshops throughout the United States and Europe. Developing a thoughtful and organized method for the left hand is fundamental to the evolution of a bassist's artistic endeavor. This theme is central to Andy's instruction to students of the double bass in their quest for instrumental mastery and musical excellence.

Acknowledgments

Along with experience and insight, writing a book takes patience. The material that you will find in these pages evolved over a long period of reflection, experimentation, and practice. Along the way there were many who directed, encouraged, and otherwise assisted me in this work as it evolved from a collection of ideas to help students learn to play jazz melodies to a formal and detailed study for the double bass. I would like to recognize Homer Mensch, Al Stauffer, and Richard Davis, teachers who guided my studies and reinforced the need to develop and internalize an organized fingering method for the left hand. It is through this process that we become free to focus on the more serious goal of making music.

I would also like to acknowledge the friends and masters including Philly Joe Jones, Chet Baker, Elvin Jones, Idris Muhammad, Michel Petrucciani, and Sue Mingus, who gave me the opportunity to develop, practice, and execute these concepts in live performance where we learn to make every note count.

And finally, special thanks to my many students who helped to clarify and refine these ideas and to my friends whose support and assistance has been instrumental in bringing this work from my music stand to yours.

Introduction

In the early days of jazz, the string bass served primarily a rhythmic function and one of the greatest challenges was just being heard. With very high action, bassists could best manage a simple, quarter-note "walking" bass line that added rhythmic drive to the chordal instrument and at the same time supplied a tonal element to the characteristic bass drum pattern. In the 1950s, as microphones and other technological innovations provided a welcome boost, jazz bassists began to explore a more melodic approach to the instrument, joining horn players as melodists playing ever more sophisticated solo lines. Milt Hinton, Oscar Pettiford, Ray Brown, and Paul Chambers were among the first to demonstrate these expanding possibilities. They began playing phrases with a shape similar to those of horn players of the day. With increasingly sophisticated lines came a demand for a more articulate and agile technique—especially for the left hand. Virtuoso skills gradually became the norm. Melodic interpretation became a requirement of any serious jazz bassist.

To meet these stringent demands, students of the double bass benefit greatly from detailed guidance about the mechanics of left-hand technique rather than using disorganized fingerings based on a limited understanding of the fingerboard. Without specific details, it is possible to gain a theoretical knowledge of jazz bass lines and solo concepts but remain technically deficient in the actual execution of those lines. The method set out in this book articulates exactly how to move the left hand: what finger to use, when to shift, when to cross strings, when to slur notes, etc. Through a systematic study of these etudes, bass students will internalize the fundamentals of a left-hand method and gradually develop confidence in finding fingering and phrasing solutions of their own.

The specific notations of the popular jazz melodies found in this book are the direct result of some fifteen years of lesson plan development for my students. This collection presents fifty compositions drawn from the classic jazz repertoire in graduated degrees of difficulty, from simple 12-bar blues themes to complicated and technically challenging chromatic lines drawn from the bebop and post-bop era. You will find explicit fingerings and phrasings designed to help you develop the fundamental techniques that generate a uniquely jazz quality in the interpretation of these melodies.

The articulations used in these studies are in standard music notation and universally recognized as the most direct and efficient way to indicate the details of string instrument playing. The underlying method is a synthesis of many sources, most notably Franz Simandl's *New Method for String Bass* (1881) and Isaia Bille's *Nuovo Metodo per Contrabbasso* (1960), two of the most respected and widely used classical method books for double bass.

Articulation Notes

Fingerings:

Many notes have a number just below the staff to indicate which finger should be used to play that note. In this example, a fingering is shown for each note. A letter placed below the fingerings and followed by a dashed line shows a group of notes to be played on the same string (measure 1: F through E♭ are played on the D string). A hyphen between fingerings (measure 2) indicates a positional shift on the fingerboard where two consecutive notes are played with the same finger.

By Miles Davis
Copyright © 1964 JAZZ HORN MUSIC CORP., SECOND FLOOR MUSIC and EAST ST. LOUIS MUSIC
Copyright Renewed
All Rights for JAZZ HORN MUSIC CORP. Controlled and Administered by SONGS OF UNIVERSAL, INC.
All Rights outside the U.S. Controlled and Administered by PRESTIGE MUSIC
All Rights Reserved   Used by Permission

Brackets:

A bracket over a group of notes indicates that those notes are to be played in the same position. Often, a fingering is given for only the first note in such a group as the remaining notes are understood to be played without any shift. In this example, the bracket implies that the B♭ in measure 3 is to be played on the D string and that the G is to be played on the open G string.

By Sonny Rollins
Copyright © 1963 Prestige Music
Copyright Renewed
International Copyright Secured   All Rights Reserved

Slurs:

The curved line connecting two or more notes indicates that those notes are to be played as a slur: Articulate only the first note with the right hand. The fingering will specify whether the slur is accomplished with a hammer-on (see measure 1 in the following example), a pull-off (measure 4), or a shift.

By Oscar Pettiford
© 1955 Orpheus Music, Inc.
Copyright Renewed
All Rights Reserved   Used by Permission

More about Slurs:

Some slurs include more than two notes and a combination of hammer-ons, pull-offs, and even open strings. In measure 3 of this example, articulate the C with your right hand, hammer on to D, pull off to C, and pull off to open G.

By Charlie Parker and Dizzy Gillespie
Copyright © 1946, Renewed 1974 and Assigned to Atlantic Music Corp. and Music Sales Corporation (ASCAP) in the U.S.
International Copyright Secured   All Rights Reserved

Bowings:

Bow strokes are notated as down-bow (⊓), moving from the frog toward the tip, and up-bow (V), moving from the tip toward the frog. Always alternate between down-bow and up-bow strokes unless otherwise indicated. Slurred notes are to be played in the same bow stroke. In the first measure of this example, D and E are played with a down-bow, A and B are played with an up-bow.

By Sonny Rollins
Copyright © 1965 Prestige Music
Copyright Renewed
International Copyright Secured   All Rights Reserved

Mordents:

A mordent indicates a trill to the diatonic tone above the specified note. The first two measures in this example are to be played as follows:

By Sonny Rollins
Copyright © 1963 Prestige Music
Copyright Renewed
International Copyright Secured   All Rights Reserved

Repeated Phrases and Sections:

Use the same fingering for each repetition of a phrase found more than once in a melody. In many song forms, an entire section is repeated. For example, when the A section is repeated after the B section, or Bridge, and identified as section C, use the same fingering for section C as indicated in section A. When these two sections are slightly different, you will find additional fingerings as needed.

Bye Bye Blackbird

Lyric by Mort Dixon
Music by Ray Henderson

Notes:
- Simple melody that can really swing.
- Entire melody can be played with very few shifts.
- Experiment with different tempos.
- Experiment with rhythmic interpretation.

© 1926 (Renewed 1953) by OLDE CLOVER LEAF MUSIC (ASCAP)/ Administered by BUG MUSIC and RAY HENDERSON (ASCAP)/ Administered by RAY HENDERSON MUSIC
All Rights Reserved   Used by Permission

Satin Doll

By Duke Ellington

Notes:
- Simple but effective ii-V harmony.
- Clever major 2nd motif throughout letter **A**.
- Pull-off to open G string in measures 6 and 24.
- Experiment with laid-back phrasing to make this melody swing.

All of Me

Words and Music by Seymour Simons and Gerald Marks

Autumn Leaves

English lyric by Johnny Mercer
French lyric by Jacques Prevert
Music by Joseph Kosma

Notes:
- Use of chord tones in melody.
- Effective repetition of rhythmic motif.
- Use of 4th (interval) across strings in letter **A**.
- Efficient and still musical fingering of F (measure 3) and E♭ (measure 5) on the A string.

© 1947, 1950 (Renewed) ENOCH ET CIE
Sole Selling Agent for U.S. and Canada: MORLEY MUSIC CO., by agreement with ENOCH ET CIE
All Rights Reserved

Yesterdays

Words by Otto Harbach
Music by Jerome Kern

Notes:
- Simple, well-constructed melody works well on the bass.
- Be careful with shift from C to F in measure 7.
- Check out alternate fingerings in letter **B**.
- Take liberties with rhythmic interpretation to make this theme your own.

Copyright © 1933 UNIVERSAL - POLYGRAM INTERNATIONAL PUBLISHING, INC.
Copyright Renewed
All Rights Reserved   Used by Permission

Blues in the Closet

By Oscar Pettiford

Notes:
- Simple but effective "riff" melody from master bassist Oscar Pettiford.
- Pull-off slur in measure 2 for stronger accent on the open G.
- Use of 3rd's harmony in the second chorus.
- Be careful with intonation of double stops.

Nardis

By Miles Davis

Notes:
- Provocative harmonic minor melody lays well on the bass.
- Play this one slightly "on top" of the beat to maintain rhythmic drive.
- Subtle harmonic motion can yield rich solo experiments.

Copyright © 1959 Jazz Horn Music Corp.
Copyright Renewed
All Rights Controlled and Administered by SONGS OF UNIVERSAL, INC.
All Rights Reserved   Used by Permission

Notes:
- Classic Duke Ellington theme works well with the bow.
- Experiment with embellishments to make this melody your own.
- Take time to play this theme with a classic swing groove.
- Practice similar phrases starting on an up-bow and down-bow (measures 1 and 3).

Solar

By Miles Davis

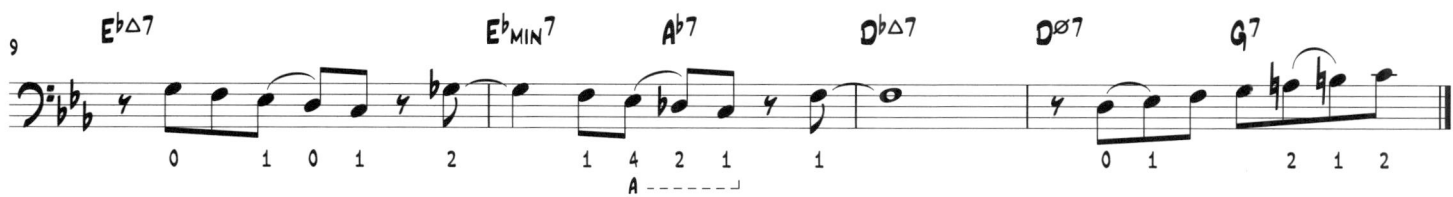

Notes:
- Be articulate with pull-offs in measures 3 and 7.
- Slur E♭ to D in measure 9, then E♭ to D♭ in measure 10.
- The shift to 1st finger on B♮ in measure 12 sets up the repeat of this theme back to measure 1.

Bass Blues
By John Coltrane

Notes:
- As played by the masterful Paul Chambers on John Coltrane's 1957 recording *Traneing In*.
- Option 2 shows the melody at an alternate position on the neck starting on the A string.

Copyright © 1957 (Renewed) JOWCOL MUSIC LLC
International Copyright Secured   All Rights Reserved

Softly as in a Morning Sunrise
from THE NEW MOON
Lyrics by Oscar Hammerstein II
Music by Sigmund Romberg

Notes:
- Play all of letter **A** in just two positions.
- Pickup in 1st ending leads to C; 2nd ending leads to B♭ going into the bridge.
- Experiment with different tempos.
- Check out Wilbur Ware's classic solo on Sonny Rollins' recording, *A Night at the Village Vanguard*.

Recorda-Me

By Joe Henderson

Notes:
- Cool bass intro played by Butch Warren on Joe Henderson's debut recording, *Page One*.
- Syncopated rhythm of intro helps to establish the groove.
- Be careful with the shift from A to D (1st finger to 2nd finger) in measure 14.
- Check out pull-off to the open G string in measure 20.

Copyright © 1963 Johen Music
Copyright Renewed
International Copyright Secured All Rights Reserved

Au Privave

By Charlie Parker

Notes:
- Interesting string crossings throughout.
- First three measures are played in one position.
- Experiment with different tempos for this Charlie Parker blues theme.

Copyright © 1956 (Renewed 1984) Atlantic Music Corp.
International Copyright Secured   All Rights Reserved

Oleo

By Sonny Rollins

Notes:
- Use open G string in measure 3 to avoid an extra shift.
- Be careful with the tricky rhythmic phrasing of this melody.
- Take your time working up to the tempo where Sonny played this.

Blue Skies

Words and Music by Irving Berlin

Notes:
- All of letter **B** is played on the G string.
- Be assertive with shift/hammer-on in measures 17 and 21 (4th finger to 1st finger).

© Copyright 1927 by Irving Berlin
Copyright Renewed
International Copyright Secured   All Rights Reserved

Scrapple from the Apple

By Charlie Parker

Notes:
- Classic Charlie Parker bebop melody works well on the bass.
- Check out cross-string fingering in measure 3.
- Work to play this one up tempo.

Copyright © 1957 (Renewed 1985) Atlantic Music Corp.
International Copyright Secured All Rights Reserved

Invitation

Words by Paul Francis Webster
Music by Bronislau Kaper

Notes:
- Fingerings in letter **A** maximize each position on the fingerboard.
- Be careful with shift in measure 9 (G♭ to F).
- Work to include melodic elements in your solo on this interesting harmonic form.

Copyright © 1952, 1956 (Renewed 1980, 1984) Webster Music Co. and EMI Robbins Music Corp.
International Copyright Secured   All Rights Reserved

Doxy

By Sonny Rollins

Notes:
- Play this one with a laid-back groove feeling.
- Trill/pull-off to open G string in measure 1.
- Triplet hammer-on/pull-off in measure 3.
- Try a little fall-off from D♭ in measure 9 and C in measure 11.

Bohemia After Dark

By Oscar Pettiford

Notes:
- Hammer-on slurs in measure 1.
- Pull-off slur in measure 4 and in 1st ending.
- Shift slur in measure 7.
- Cool slur/pull-off to open G string in measure 26.

© 1955 Orpheus Music, Inc.
Copyright Renewed
All Rights Reserved   Used by Permission

Dig

By Miles Davis

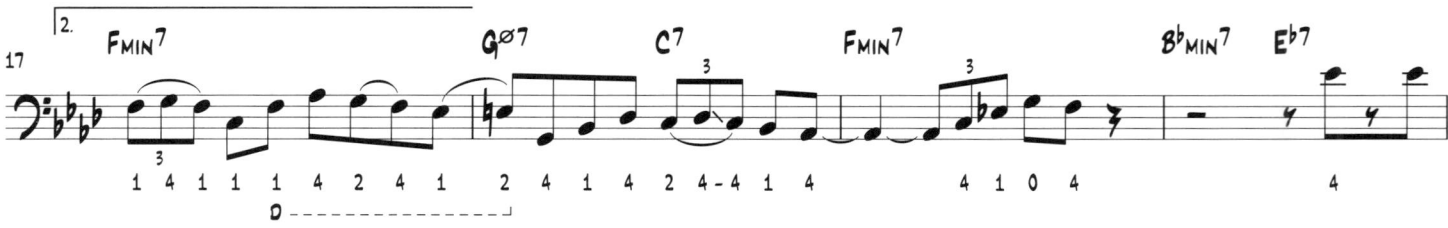

Notes:
- First seven measures are played in one position.
- Check out shift slur in measures 9 and 10.
- Don't be intimidated by simple D♭△9 arpeggio in measure 11.
- Be assertive with slur in measure 17 (G to F).

Copyright © 1964 JAZZ HORN MUSIC CORP., SECOND FLOOR MUSIC and EAST ST. LOUIS MUSIC
Copyright Renewed
All Rights for JAZZ HORN MUSIC CORP. Controlled and Administered by SONGS OF UNIVERSAL, INC.
All Rights outside the U.S. Controlled and Administered by PRESTIGE MUSIC
All Rights Reserved Used by Permission

Billie's Bounce (Bill's Bounce)

By Charlie Parker

Notes:
- Slurs across strings are possible with the bow (measure 4).
- Remember A♯ to A♭ in measure 5.
- Cool chromatic line in measure 8.
- Check out slurs in measure 10.

Copyright © 1945 (Renewed 1973) Atlantic Music Corp.
All Rights for the World excluding the U.S. Controlled and Administered by Screen Gems-EMI Music Inc.
International Copyright Secured   All Rights Reserved

A Night In Tunisia

By John "Dizzy" Gillespie and Frank Paparelli

Notes:
- In second measure of intro, play F on the A string to minimize shifts.
- Be assertive with double hammer-on slur at start of letter **A**.

Copyright © 1944 UNIVERSAL MUSIC CORP.
Copyright Renewed
All Rights Reserved   Used by Permission

Lullaby of Birdland

Words by George David Weiss
Music by George Shearing

Notes:
- Interesting moving line on A string in measures 6–8.
- Be assertive with hammer-on slur in measures 11 and 13, and slur to C in measure 18.
- Check your intonation in measure 13 (B♭ on D string to B♮ on G string).

© 1952, 1954 (Renewed 1980, 1982) EMI LONGITUDE MUSIC
All Rights Reserved   International Copyright Secured   Used by Permission

Goodbye Pork Pie Hat

By Charles Mingus

Notes:
- Mingus' soulful tribute to saxophonist Lester Young works well on the bass.
- E♭ minor blues scale is used for almost the entire melody.
- Try a solo on this altered minor blues form as indicated.

Copyright © 1975 JAZZ WORKSHOP, INC. and FLYING RED RHINO
Copyright Renewed
All Rights for FLYING RED RHINO in the U.S. Controlled and Administered by SPIRIT ONE MUSIC
International Copyright Secured   All Rights Reserved

Interplay

Music by Bill Evans

Notes:
- Creative, melodic use of a simple diatonic scale.
- Useful as a cross-string study.
- Check pull-off to open G string in measures 2, 10, and 11.
- Be assertive with slurs in the last 2 measures.

Lament

By J.J. Johnson

Notes:
- Lyrical, melodic line lays well on the instrument.
- Be careful to play bowings as indicated.
- Play last beat of measures 1 and 2 close to the frog.
- Experiment with rhythmic expression throughout.

© 1954 (Renewed 1982) SCREEN GEMS-EMI MUSIC INC.
All Rights Reserved   International Copyright Secured   Used by Permission

Tail Feathers
Written by Ron Carter

Notes:
- Medium groove gem from the masterful Ron Carter.
- In measure 7, the D is first played on the D string and then on the G string.
- Be assertive with pull-off/shift in measures 10 and 16.
- Check out cool whole-tone line in measure 12–13.

Copyright © 1981 RETRAC PRODUCTIONS, INC.
International Copyright Secured   All Rights Reserved

Lester Left Town

By Wayne Shorter

Notes:
- Rhythmic 2-1 fingering in first two measures.
- Be assertive with shift/slur on the D string in measures 11–12 (B♭ to G♭).
- In measure 31, play B♭ on the G string, then on the D string.
- Work to solo on this tricky harmonic form.

In Walked Bud

By Thelonious Monk

Notes:
- Play B♮ in measures 4 and 6 with 2nd finger to set up the next measure.
- Clever use of chromatic approach tones in letter **A**.
- Cool hammer-on/pull-off in letter **B**.
- Check out double-stop/triple-stop in measures 12 and 13. Try to sustain the C♭ through both measures.

Copyright © 1948 (Renewed) by Embassy Music Corporation (BMI)
International Copyright Secured   All Rights Reserved
Reprinted by Permission

Four

By Miles Davis

Notes:
- Hammer-on from open G string in measures 9 and 13.
- Pull-off to open G string in measures 11 and 15.
- Be articulate with shift in measure 17 (E–D♯) which sets up the end of this line.

Copyright © 1963 Prestige Music
Copyright Renewed
International Copyright Secured   All Rights Reserved

In a Sentimental Mood

By Duke Ellington

Well You Needn't (It's Over Now)

Words by Mike Ferro
Music by Thelonious Monk

Notes:
- Good study for practicing hammer-on slurs.
- Good study for barring across strings.
- Be assertive with shift from F to E♭ in measures 1–2.
- Be careful with intonation through chromatic harmony of letter **B**.

Copyright © 1944 (Renewed) by Regent Music Corporation (BMI)
International Copyright Secured All Rights Reserved
Used by Permission

I Remember Clifford

By Benny Golson

Israel

By John Carisi

Notes:
- Cool minor blues melody with slightly altered changes.
- Begins in thumb position (+ = thumb).
- Keep your thumb anchored for pull-off in measure 2.
- In measure 6, play the octave G closed to make slur more effective.
- Be assertive with shift from E to A♭ in measure 12.

Ray's Idea

By Walter Gil Fuller and Raymond Brown

Notes:
- Be assertive with shift to G♭ (4th finger) in measures 7, 9, and 25.
- Check out recordings by Dizzy Gillespie's big band in the '40s with Ray Brown on bass.
- Miles played this bebop classic in the key of F on recordings from the '50s.

Copyright © 1947 (Renewed) by Music Sales Corporation (ASCAP)
International Copyright Secured   All Rights Reserved

Afternoon in Paris

By John Lewis

Epistrophy

By Thelonious Monk and Kenny Clarke

Notes:
- Quirky Monk classic using minor 2nd and augmented 5th intervals.
- Be careful with E to C shift in measures 5, 9, and 25.
- Try improvising on this tricky chromatic harmony.

Copyright © 1947 (Renewed 1975) by Embassy Music Corporation (BMI) and Music Sales Corporation (ASCAP)
International Copyright Secured   All Rights Reserved
Reprinted by Permission

Ornithology

By Charlie Parker and Bennie Harris

Notes:
- Be assertive with triplet pull-off in measure 1.
- Stretch to play the triplet figure in 1st and 2nd endings without any real shift.

Bloomdido

By Charlie Parker

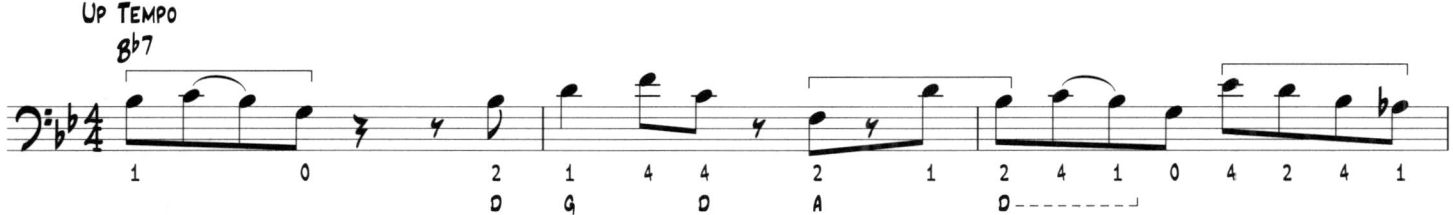

Notes:
- This melody is more complicated than it first appears.
- Be assertive with the shift/hammer-on in measure 4 (F to C).
- Cool cross-string fingering in measure 8.
- Stylized closing riff in measure 11.

Copyright © 1953 (Renewed 1981) Atlantic Music Corp.
International Copyright Secured All Rights Reserved

Pent Up House

By Sonny Rollins

Notes:
- Play measures 2-4 across the strings without any shift.
- Last three notes in measure 9 are played on the D string to set up the next two measures.
- Be careful with alternating major 3rd/minor 3rd intervals central to this theme.

Receipt Please

Written by Ron Carter

Notes:
- Fun and quirky 20-bar theme from master bassist Ron Carter.
- Be careful with consecutive 4ths in measures 7 and 8.
- Practice slowly at first to get a sense for the entire piece.

Along Came Betty

By Benny Golson

Notes:
- Check out the shift/slur in measure 5.
- Pull-off to open G string in measure 12.
- Diminished arpeggio on F7 in measure 18.
- Try working up a solo on this very tricky harmonic form.

Copyright © 1958 (Renewed 1986) IBBOB MUSIC, INC. d/b/a TIME STEP MUSIC (ASCAP)
International Copyright Secured   All Rights Reserved

Teen Town

By Jaco Pastorius

Notes:
- Post-bop bass melody from the masterful Jaco Pastorius.
- Great example of a line that is well suited to the instrument.
- Each phrase can be played with very few shifts.
- Be careful with rhythmic articulation to make this line work.

Copyright © 1977 Haapala Music
Copyright Renewed
All Rights Reserved   Used by Permission

Milestones
By Miles Davis

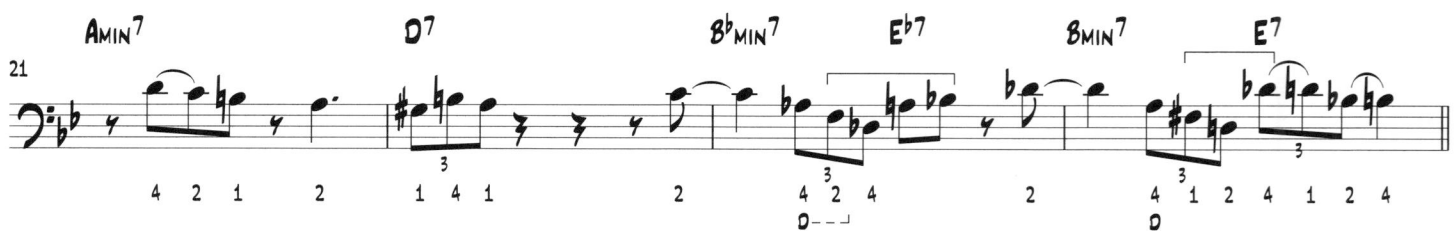

Notes:
- Interesting string crossings in measures 9, 13, and 15 (B♭ on the D string).
- Be careful to articulate slurs in measures 12 and 28.
- Play F in measure 23 with 2nd finger.
- Check out shift/hammer-on in measure 24 (D♭ to D♮).

The Girl from Ipanema (Garôta de Ipanema)

Music by Antonio Carlos Jobim
English Words by Norman Gimbel
Original Words by Vinicius de Moraes

Notes:
- This melody is to be played one octave higher than written.
- All of letter **A** is played on the G string.
- Have fun with the very syncopated rhythms of this line.

Copyright © 1963 ANTONIO CARLOS JOBIM and VINICIUS DE MORAES, Brazil
Copyright Renewed 1991 and Assigned to SONGS OF UNIVERSAL, INC. and WORDS WEST LLC
English Words Renewed 1991 by NORMAN GIMBEL for the World and Assigned to WORDS WEST LLC (P.O. Box 15187, Beverly Hills, CA 90209 USA)
All Rights Reserved   Used by Permission

My One and Only Love

Words by Robert Mellin
Music by Guy Wood

Notes:
- Great lyrical quality in an almost entirely diatonic melody.
- Be careful with shift from E to B in measure 1 and octave shift at letter **B**.
- Keep thumb anchored on octave in measures 4 and 5.
- If necessary, try this theme one octave lower to get a sense of the line.

© 1952, 1953 (Renewed 1980, 1981) EMI MUSIC PUBLISHING LTD. and WAROCK CORP.
All Rights for EMI MUSIC PUBLISHING LTD. Controlled and Administered by COLGEMS-EMI MUSIC INC.
All Rights Reserved   International Copyright Secured   Used by Permission

Anthropology

By Charlie Parker and Dizzy Gillespie

Notes:
- Be assertive with shift/hammer-on from third to fourth measure (1st to 4th finger).
- Hammer-on/pull-off combination on first beat of 2nd ending and in measures 16 and 25.
- Anchor thumb on F♯ going into letter **B**.

Copyright © 1946, Renewed 1974 and Assigned to Atlantic Music Corp. and Music Sales Corporation (ASCAP) in the U.S.
International Copyright Secured   All Rights Reserved

Confirmation

By Charlie Parker

Notes:
- Check out gliss in measure 7.
- Be sure to play hammer-on/pull-off to open G in time (measure 18).
- Be articulate with string crossings in measure 21.
- 1-1-1 fingering in measure 30 helps slur swing the most.

Copyright © 1946 (Renewed 1974) Atlantic Music Corp.
International Copyright Secured All Rights Reserved

Self-Portrait in Three Colors
By Charles Mingus

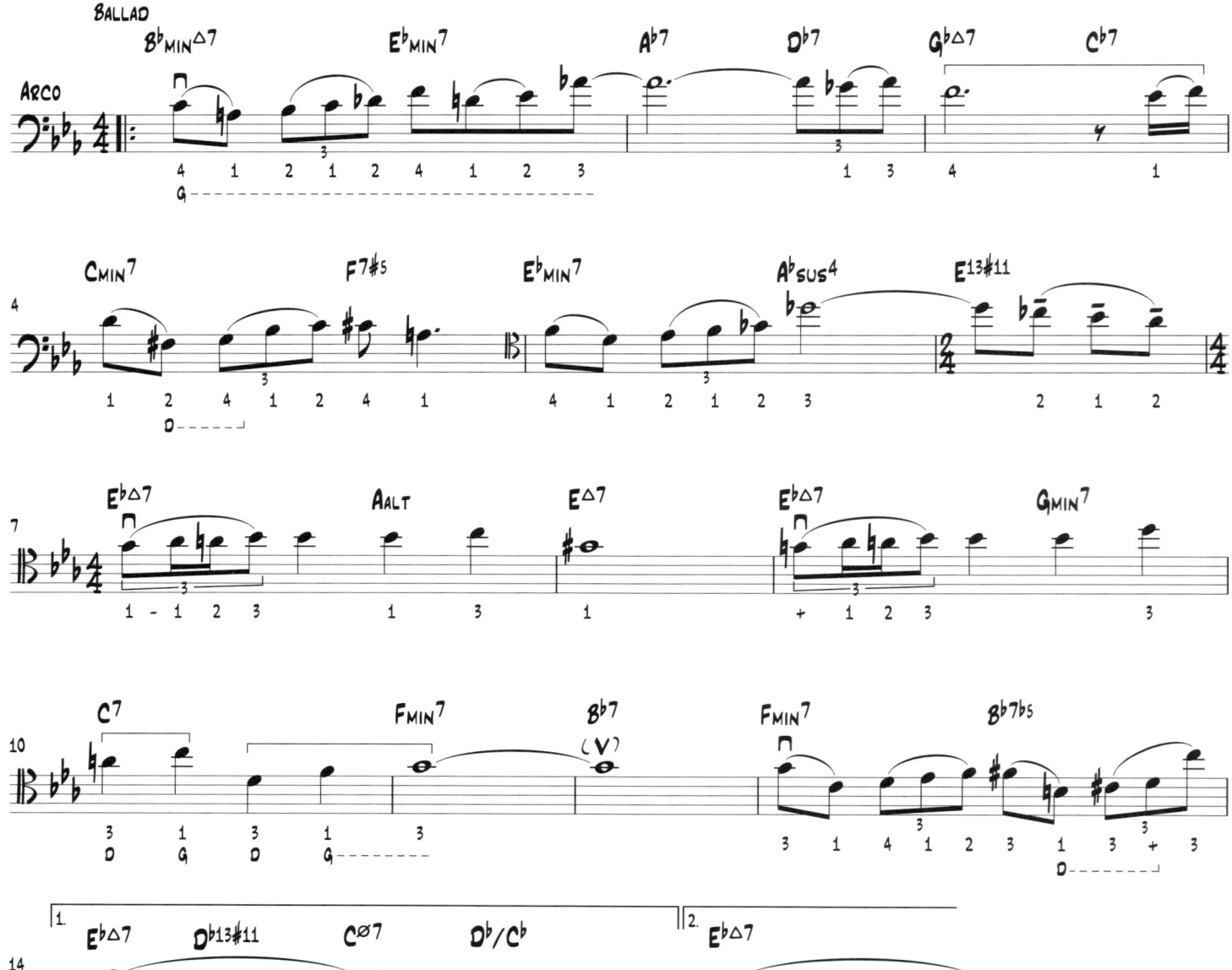

Notes:
- Play this lyrical Mingus theme entirely on the G string except where indicated.
- Be careful with upper register written in tenor clef.
- Check out the effective countermelodies on the original recording, *Mingus Ah Um*.

Moose the Mooch

By Charlie Parker

Notes:
- Be articulate with pull-off slurs to open G string in measures 2, 8, and 10.
- Check out cross-string fingering in measure 2.
- Bridge can be played in just three different positions.

Copyright © 1946 (Renewed 1974) Atlantic Music Corp.
International Copyright Secured   All Rights Reserved

The Best-Selling Jazz Book of All Time Is Now Legal!

The Real Books are the most popular jazz books of all time. Since the 1970s, musicians have trusted these volumes to get them through every gig, night after night. The problem is that the books were illegally produced and distributed, without any regard to copyright law, or royalties paid to the composers who created these musical masterpieces.

Hal Leonard is very proud to present the first legitimate and legal editions of these books ever produced. You won't even notice the difference, other than all the notorious errors being fixed: the covers and typeface look the same, the song lists are nearly identical, and the price for our edition is even cheaper than the originals!

Every conscientious musician will appreciate that these books are now produced accurately and ethically, benefitting the songwriters that we owe for some of the greatest tunes of all time!

VOLUME 1
Includes: Autumn Leaves • Body and Soul • Don't Get Around Much Anymore • Falling in Love with Love • Have You Met Miss Jones? • Lullaby of Birdland • Misty • Satin Doll • Stella by Starlight • and hundreds more!
00240221	C Edition	$29.99
00240224	B♭ Edition	$29.95
00240225	E♭ Edition	$29.99
00240226	Bass Clef Edition	$29.95
00240292	C Edition 6 x 9	$27.95
00451087	C Edition on CD-ROM	$25.00

VOLUME 2
Includes: Avalon • Birdland • Come Rain or Come Shine • Fever • Georgia on My Mind • It Might as Well Be Spring • Moonglow • The Nearness of You • On the Sunny Side of the Street • Route 66 • Sentimental Journey • Smoke Gets in Your Eyes • Tangerine • Yardbird Suite • and more!
00240222	C Edition	$29.99
00240227	B♭ Edition	$29.95
00240228	E♭ Edition	$29.95
00240229	Bass Clef Edition	$29.95
00240293	C Edition 6 x 9	$27.95

VOLUME 3
Includes: Ain't Misbehavin' • Cheek to Cheek • The Lady Is a Tramp • A Nightingale Sang in Berkeley Square • On a Clear Day • Stormy Weather • The Very Thought of You • and more!
00240233	C Edition	$29.99
00240284	B♭ Edition	$29.95
00240285	E♭ Edition	$29.95
00240286	Bass Clef Edition	$29.95

VOLUME 4
Includes: The Best Is Yet to Come • A Foggy Day (In London Town) • I Got Rhythm • Kansas City • Night and Day • Ol' Man River • Smile • Them There Eyes • and more!
00240296	C Edition	$29.99

Play-along CDs to some of the most popular songs featured in the world famous *Real Books* are available. Each volume features selections sorted alphabetically from the 6th edition, each in 3-CD sets.

The Real Book Play-Along – Volume 1
00240302	A-D	$24.99
00240303	E-J	$24.95
00240304	L-R	$24.95
00240305	S-Z	$24.99

The Real Book Play-Along – Volume 2
00240351	A-D	$24.99
00240352	E-I	$24.99
00240353	J-R	$24.99
00240354	S-Z	$24.99

Also available:
00240264	The Real Blues Book	$34.99
00240306	The Real Christmas Book	$25.00
00240137	Miles Davis Real Book	$19.95
00240235	The Duke Ellington Real Book	$19.99
00240331	The Bud Powell Real Book	$19.99
00240313	The Real Rock Book	$29.99
00240359	The Real Tab Book – Vol. 1	$32.50
00310910	The Real Bluegrass Book	$29.99
00240355	The Real Dixieland Book	$29.99
00240317	The Real Worship Book	$29.99

THE REAL VOCAL BOOK
00240230	Volume 1 High Voice	$29.95
00240307	Volume 1 Low Voice	$29.99
00240231	Volume 2 High Voice	$29.95
00240308	Volume 2 Low Voice	$29.95

THE REAL BOOK – STAFF PAPER
00240327	$9.95

Complete song lists online at www.halleonard.com
Prices and availability subject to change without notice.

For More Information, See Your Local Music Dealer, Or Write To:

7777 W. Bluemound Rd. P.O. Box 13819 Milwaukee, WI 53213

Presenting the Hal Leonard JAZZ PLAY-ALONG SERIES

For use with all B-flat, E-flat, Bass Clef and C instruments, the Jazz Play-Along® Series is the ultimate learning tool for all jazz musicians. With musician-friendly lead sheets, melody cues, and other split-track choices on the included CD, these first-of-a-kind packages help you master improvisation while playing some of the greatest tunes of all time. FOR STUDY, each tune includes a split track with: melody cue with proper style and inflection • professional rhythm tracks • choruses for soloing • removable bass part • removable piano part. FOR PERFORMANCE, each tune also has: an additional full stereo accompaniment track (no melody) • additional choruses for soloing.

1. **DUKE ELLINGTON**
00841644................$16.95

1A. **MAIDEN VOYAGE/ALL BLUES**
00843158................$15.99

2. **MILES DAVIS**
00841645................$16.95

3. **THE BLUES**
00841646................$16.99

4. **JAZZ BALLADS**
00841691................$16.99

5. **BEST OF BEBOP**
00841689................$16.99

6. **JAZZ CLASSICS WITH EASY CHANGES**
00841690................$16.99

7. **ESSENTIAL JAZZ STANDARDS**
00843000................$16.99

8. **ANTONIO CARLOS JOBIM AND THE ART OF THE BOSSA NOVA**
00843001................$16.95

9. **DIZZY GILLESPIE**
00843002................$16.99

10. **DISNEY CLASSICS**
00843003................$16.99

11. **RODGERS AND HART FAVORITES**
00843004................$16.99

12. **ESSENTIAL JAZZ CLASSICS**
00843005................$16.99

13. **JOHN COLTRANE**
00843006................$16.95

14. **IRVING BERLIN**
00843007................$15.99

15. **RODGERS & HAMMERSTEIN**
00843008................$15.99

16. **COLE PORTER**
00843009................$15.95

17. **COUNT BASIE**
00843010................$16.95

18. **HAROLD ARLEN**
00843011................$15.95

19. **COOL JAZZ**
00843012................$15.95

20. **CHRISTMAS CAROLS**
00843080................$14.95

21. **RODGERS AND HART CLASSICS**
00843014................$14.95

22. **WAYNE SHORTER**
00843015................$16.95

23. **LATIN JAZZ**
00843016................$16.95

24. **EARLY JAZZ STANDARDS**
00843017................$14.95

25. **CHRISTMAS JAZZ**
00843018................$16.95

26. **CHARLIE PARKER**
00843019................$16.95

27. **GREAT JAZZ STANDARDS**
00843020................$15.99

28. **BIG BAND ERA**
00843021................$15.99

29. **LENNON AND MCCARTNEY**
00843022................$16.95

30. **BLUES' BEST**
00843023................$15.99

31. **JAZZ IN THREE**
00843024................$15.99

32. **BEST OF SWING**
00843025................$15.99

33. **SONNY ROLLINS**
00843029................$15.95

34. **ALL TIME STANDARDS**
00843030................$15.99

35. **BLUESY JAZZ**
00843031................$15.99

36. **HORACE SILVER**
00843032................$16.99

37. **BILL EVANS**
00843033................$16.95

38. **YULETIDE JAZZ**
00843034................$16.95

39. **"ALL THE THINGS YOU ARE" & MORE JEROME KERN SONGS**
00843035................$15.99

40. **BOSSA NOVA**
00843036................$15.99

41. **CLASSIC DUKE ELLINGTON**
00843037................$16.99

42. **GERRY MULLIGAN FAVORITES**
00843038................$16.99

43. **GERRY MULLIGAN CLASSICS**
00843039................$16.95

44. **OLIVER NELSON**
00843040................$16.95

45. **JAZZ AT THE MOVIES**
00843041................$15.99

46. **BROADWAY JAZZ STANDARDS**
00843042................$15.99

47. **CLASSIC JAZZ BALLADS**
00843043................$15.99

48. **BEBOP CLASSICS**
00843044................$16.99

49. **MILES DAVIS STANDARDS**
00843045................$16.95

50. **GREAT JAZZ CLASSICS**
00843046................$15.99

51. **UP-TEMPO JAZZ**
00843047................$15.99

52. **STEVIE WONDER**
00843048................$15.95

53. **RHYTHM CHANGES**
00843049................$15.99

54. **"MOONLIGHT IN VERMONT" AND OTHER GREAT STANDARDS**
00843050................$15.99

55. **BENNY GOLSON**
00843052................$15.95

56. "GEORGIA ON MY MIND" & OTHER SONGS BY HOAGY CARMICHAEL
00843056 .... $15.99

57. VINCE GUARALDI
00843057 .... $16.99

58. MORE LENNON AND MCCARTNEY
00843059 .... $15.99

59. SOUL JAZZ
00843060 .... $15.99

60. DEXTER GORDON
00843061 .... $15.95

61. MONGO SANTAMARIA
00843062 .... $15.95

62. JAZZ-ROCK FUSION
00843063 .... $14.95

63. CLASSICAL JAZZ
00843064 .... $14.95

64. TV TUNES
00843065 .... $14.95

65. SMOOTH JAZZ
00843066 .... $16.99

66. A CHARLIE BROWN CHRISTMAS
00843067 .... $16.99

67. CHICK COREA
00843068 .... $15.95

68. CHARLES MINGUS
00843069 .... $16.95

69. CLASSIC JAZZ
00843071 .... $15.99

70. THE DOORS
00843072 .... $14.95

71. COLE PORTER CLASSICS
00843073 .... $14.95

72. CLASSIC JAZZ BALLADS
00843074 .... $15.99

73. JAZZ/BLUES
00843075 .... $14.95

74. BEST JAZZ CLASSICS
00843076 .... $15.99

75. PAUL DESMOND
00843077 .... $14.95

76. BROADWAY JAZZ BALLADS
00843078 .... $15.99

77. JAZZ ON BROADWAY
00843079 .... $15.99

78. STEELY DAN
00843070 .... $14.99

79. MILES DAVIS CLASSICS
00843081 .... $15.99

80. JIMI HENDRIX
00843083 .... $15.99

81. FRANK SINATRA – CLASSICS
00843084 .... $15.99

82. FRANK SINATRA – STANDARDS
00843085 .... $15.99

83. ANDREW LLOYD WEBBER
00843104 .... $14.95

84. BOSSA NOVA CLASSICS
00843105 .... $14.95

85. MOTOWN HITS
00843109 .... $14.95

86. BENNY GOODMAN
00843110 .... $14.95

87. DIXIELAND
00843111 .... $14.95

88. DUKE ELLINGTON FAVORITES
00843112 .... $14.95

89. IRVING BERLIN FAVORITES
00843113 .... $14.95

90. THELONIOUS MONK CLASSICS
00841262 .... $16.99

91. THELONIOUS MONK FAVORITES
00841263 .... $16.99

92. LEONARD BERNSTEIN
00450134 .... $15.99

93. DISNEY FAVORITES
00843142 .... $14.99

94. RAY
00843143 .... $14.99

95. JAZZ AT THE LOUNGE
00843144 .... $14.99

96. LATIN JAZZ STANDARDS
00843145 .... $14.99

97. MAYBE I'M AMAZED
00843148 .... $15.99

98. DAVE FRISHBERG
00843149 .... $15.99

99. SWINGING STANDARDS
00843150 .... $14.99

100. LOUIS ARMSTRONG
00740423 .... $15.99

101. BUD POWELL
00843152 .... $14.99

102. JAZZ POP
00843153 .... $14.99

103. ON GREEN DOLPHIN STREET & OTHER JAZZ CLASSICS
00843154 .... $14.99

104. ELTON JOHN
00843155 .... $14.99

105. SOULFUL JAZZ
00843151 .... $15.99

106. SLO' JAZZ
00843117 .... $14.99

107. MOTOWN CLASSICS
00843116 .... $14.99

108. JAZZ WALTZ
00843159 .... $15.99

109. OSCAR PETERSON
00843160 .... $15.99

110. JUST STANDARDS
00843161 .... $15.99

111. COOL CHRISTMAS
00843162 .... $15.99

114. MODERN JAZZ QUARTET FAVORITES
00843163 .... $15.99

115. THE SOUND OF MUSIC
00843164 .... $15.99

116. JACO PASTORIUS
00843165 .... $15.99

117. ANTONIO CARLOS JOBIM – MORE HITS
00843166 .... $15.99

118. BIG JAZZ STANDARDS COLLECTION
00843167 .... $27.50

119. JELLY ROLL MORTON
00843168 .... $15.99

120. J.S. BACH
00843169 .... $15.99

121. DJANGO REINHARDT
00843170 .... $15.99

122. PAUL SIMON
00843182 .... $16.99

123. BACHARACH & DAVID
00843185 .... $15.99

124. JAZZ-ROCK HORN HITS
00843186 .... $15.99

126. COUNT BASIE CLASSICS
00843157 .... $15.99

Prices, contents, and availability subject to change without notice.

FOR MORE INFORMATION, SEE YOUR LOCAL MUSIC DEALER, OR WRITE TO:

HAL•LEONARD® CORPORATION
7777 W. BLUEMOUND RD. P.O. BOX 13819
MILWAUKEE, WISCONSIN 53213

For complete songlists and more, visit Hal Leonard online at
www.halleonard.com